Unni Leela Lakshmi Ach Al
Ullaska

C0-DUQ-648

Wings of Fire
AN AUTOBIOGRAPHY

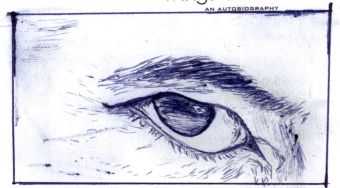

APJ ABDUL KALAM was born in 1931 to a little-educated family of boat-owners in Rameswaram, Tamilnadu. He went on to have an unparalleled career as a scientist in India, culminating in the receipt of India's highest civilian award, the Bharat Ratna.

As mission director in the launch of SLV-3, India's first satellite launch vehicle, and later, as chief of the country's defence research and development programme, he realised the potential for dynamism and innovation in India's research establishments. This is as much the story of Dr. Kalam's own rise from obscurity and his personal and professional struggles, as it is the saga of independent India's struggle for self-reliance in defence technology.

Dr. Kalam was sworn in as the eleventh President of India on 25 July 2002.

Wings of Fire
AN AUTOBIOGRAPHY

APJ Abdul Kalam
with Arun Tiwari

Simplified and abridged by Mukul Chowdhry

Universities Press

Universities Press (India) Private Limited

Registered Office
3-5-819 Hyderguda, Hyderabad 500 029 (A.P), India
E-mail : hyd2_upilco@ sancharnet.in

Distributed by
Orient Longman Private Limited

Registered Office
3-6-752, Himayatnagar, Hyderabad 500 029 (A.P) India

Other Offices
Bangalore/Bhopal/Bhubaneswar/Chandigarh/Chennai
Ernakulam/Guwahati/Hyderabad/Jaipur/Kolkata/Lucknow
/Mumbai/New Delhi/Patna

©Universities Press (India) Private Limited 2004

First Published 2004

Reprinted at 2005

ISBN 81 7371 518 1

Typeset by
Trinity Designers & Typesetters
Chennai 600 041

Printed in India at
Orion Printers Private Limited
Hyderabad 500 004

Published by
Universities Press (India) Private Limited
3-5-819 Hyderguda, Hyderabad 500 029 (AP), India

A NOTE BY THE AUTHOR

When I first began the reminiscences that have gone into this book, I was uncertain which of my memories were worth narrating. My childhood is precious to me, but would it be of any revelance to anyone else?

Was it worth the reader's while, I wondered, to know of the trials and triumphs of a small-town boy? Of the straitened circumstances of my schooldays and the odd jobs I worked to pay my school fees? Of how my decision to turn vegetarian was partly due to my financial constraints as a college student? Of my frustrated attempt to become a pilot in the Indian Air Force? Or how I became a rocket engineer instead of the civil servant my father dreamed I would be? Why would any of this be of interest to the general reader, I wondered.

Finally, I was convinced that my story was relevant, if not for anything else but because it tells the story of an individual destiny, which cannot be seen in isolation from the social matrix in which it is embedded. I decided to describe the individuals who had had a profound influence on my life. This book is by way of thanks, therefore, to my parents and immediate family, and to the teachers and mentors I was fortunate to have had as a young student and in my professional life.

This story is not just an account of my personal triumphs and tribulations. It tells of the successes and setbacks of the scientific establishment in modern India, struggling to establish itself on the technological forefront. It is a tribute to the unflagging enthusiasm and capabilities of my young colleagues, who helped realise our collective dreams. The saga of India's search for scientific self-sufficiency and technological competence is a parable for our times.

We are all born with a divine fire in us. Our effort should be to give wings to this fire.

May God bless you!

APJ Abdul Kalam

CONTENTS

1. STRONG ROOTS

I was born into a middle-class Tamil family, in the island town of Rameswaram. It was 1931, and Rameswaram was a part of Madras State, in British India. I was one of many children—a short boy with rather ordinary looks, born to tall and handsome parents.

My father, Jainulabdeen, was neither highly educated nor very rich. But these were not disadvantages, since he was wise and possessed a truly generous spirit. My mother, Ashiamma, came from a more distinguished family—one of her ancestors had been given the title of 'Bahadur' by the British. Her generosity equalled my father's—I do not remember the number of people my mother fed every day, but I am quite certain that far more outsiders ate with us than all the members of our large family put together! My parents were widely regarded as an ideal couple.

Mine was a very secure childhood, both materially and emotionally. My father lived frugally, according to his austere principles. His day started with the morning namaaz, which he observed just before dawn. He avoided comforts and luxuries— things he considered non-essential. Essential needs—food, medicine and clothes—were well-provided for. I normally ate with my mother, sitting on the floor of the kitchen. She would place a banana leaf before me, on which she ladled rice and hot, mouth-watering sambhar, a variety of sharp, home-made pickles and a dollop of fresh coconut chutney.

We lived in our ancestral house, built of limestone and brick in the middle of the nineteenth century. It was a fairly large house, situated in Rameswaram's Mosque Street.

The famous Shiva temple, which made Rameswaram so sacred to pilgrims, was about a ten-minute walk from our house. Our locality was predominantly Muslim; in fact, Mosque Street was named after a very old mosque in the area. People of both religions, Hinduism and Islam, lived amicably as neighbours—a result of having the two shrines side by side.

The high priest of the temple, Pakshi Lakshmana Sastry, was a very close friend of my father's. One of the clearest memories of my early childhood is of the two men, each in his traditional attire, discussing spiritual matters. The similarities in their thinking rose above the differences in their modes of worship.

As a child, my father would take me for evening prayers to the mosque. I would hear the Arabic prayers being chanted, without the faintest idea of what they meant. But I was totally convinced that the prayers reached God. When I was old enough to ask questions, I asked my father about prayer and its relevance in communicating with God. He explained that there was nothing mysterious or complicated about praying.

"When you pray," he said, "you move beyond your body and its material concerns. You become a part of the cosmos, where wealth, age, caste, and creed are not standards for dividing people."

Often, when my father left the mosque after prayers, people of different religions would be sitting outside, waiting for him. Many of them offered bowls of water for him to dip his fingertips and say a prayer. This water was then carried home for invalids. I also remember people visiting our home to offer thanks after being cured. My father, in his unpretentious way, asked them to thank Allah, the benevolent and merciful.

My father was able to express complex spiritual concepts in such simple Tamil that even a child like me could understand them. He once told me that every human being, in his or her own time, place and situation—be it good or bad—becomes a part of the divine being that we call God. Troubles and adversity come to teach us, and to jolt us out of complacency and self-conceit.

I asked my father why he didn't say all this to the numerous people who came to him for help and advice. He was silent for a while, as if trying to assess how much I was capable of understanding. When he replied, it was in a low quiet voice, and I felt greatly energised by his words.

He said that whenever human beings find themselves alone or in distress, they look for company—help and consolation of some kind. Every suffering or desire, pain or hope, finds a special helper. My father considered himself just that—a helper, a go-between who used the power of prayer, worship or offerings to defeat evil, self-destructive forces. But, he believed this to be the wrong approach to solving problems, because prayer of this sort emanated from fear. He believed that one's destiny should be a vision borne out of true knowledge of the self, and that fear often prevents one's hopes from being fulfilled. I knew as I heard him that I was lucky to be the person to whom he explained all this.

I was greatly influenced by my father's philosophy. I now believe, and I did even as a child, that once a person breaks the emotional shackles that hold him or her back, the road to personal freedom is only a short step ahead. Happiness and peace of mind come to us from within, and not from external sources. Once a person knows this, setbacks and hurdles become temporary.

I was very young—just six years old—when I saw my father put his philosophy into practice. He decided to build a sail boat to ferry pilgrims from Rameswaram to Dhanuskodi and back. I watched the wooden boat being built on the seashore; timber was seasoned over wood-fires to make the hull and the bulkheads. It was fascinating to watch the boat take shape.

When the boat was ready my father started a brisk business. Some time later, a severe cyclone struck the Rameswaram coast. Our boat was wrecked in the strong winds. My father bore his loss with composure—in fact, he was more concerned about a greater tragedy caused by the gale. The Pamban bridge had collapsed during the cyclonic storm, when a train full of passengers was crossing over it.

I learnt from both my father's attitude and the actual disaster. Till then I had only experienced the beauty of the sea; now its force and uncontrollable energy stood revealed.

2.   EARLY INFLUENCES

A relative of ours, Ahmed Jallaluddin, had helped my father when he built the boat. Later, he married my sister, Zohara. When the boat was being built and then later while it was plying, Jallaluddin and I became good friends, despite the age difference. He was fifteen years older than I, and called me Azad.

Every evening we went for long walks together. We usually talked about spiritual matters. The atmosphere of Rameswaram, with so many pilgrims coming to worship, probably inspired our interest. Our first sight was usually of the huge, impressive Shiva temple. We would circle it with the same reverence as a pilgrim from a distant place.

Jallaluddin seemed to be able to communicate directly with God, almost as if they were partners working together. He would talk to God about all his doubts, as if God were standing right beside him and listening. I found this method of communication intriguing. I also observed pilgrims dipping themselves in the sea, chanting their ancient prayers and performing rituals.

The sense of respect for an unknown and unseen force was very apparent—in them and in him.

Jallaluddin had not had much schooling, because his family had not been able to afford his higher education. That was probably why he always encouraged me to excel. He seemed to get a great deal of satisfaction from my academic success. Incidentally, at that time, Jallaluddin was the only person on the island who could write in English. He wrote letters for just about everyone who needed it—applications, official letters or personal letters. And, few people in the neighbourhood could match him in his knowledge and awareness of the world outside our own little one.

Jallaluddin was a major influence on my life at that stage. He talked to me about many things—scientific discoveries, contemporary writing and literature, even medical science and the strides it was making. More than anyone even, it was he who helped me look beyond the limited horizons of my life.

Another aspect of my life then was a growing love for reading, a habit which has endured all my life. In our way of life, books would have been rare and difficult to obtain—if it were not for the huge personal library of STR Manickam. Manickam was a militant nationalist, someone who wanted to fight for Independence by means other than the Gandhian way of non-violence. I often visited his home to borrow books and he always encouraged me to read more.

There was yet another person who helped shape my boyhood— my cousin, Samsuddin. He was the only distributor for newspapers in Rameswaram. The morning train from Pamban brought in the Tamil newspapers for Rameswaram's thousand or so literate people. The newspapers then used to be filled with the latest developments in the struggle for Independence, something most people were avidly interested in.

Discussions on Adolf Hitler, Mahatma Gandhi and Mohammed Ali Jinnah were held by those who had a wider world-view. Most people were deeply interested in, or committed to, the political movement against high-caste Hindus started by Periyar EV Ramaswamy. *Dinamani* was the most popular newspaper in those days. Of course, I was not able to decipher the printed matter then, and had to be content with simply looking at the pictures in the papers before Samsuddin delivered them.

I was eight years old when World War II started in 1939. Jallaluddin would tell me of incidents in the war and I would later try to trace and recreate them in the headlines of *Dinamani*. The war, which cost so many millions their lives, was to influence me, although not directly, in different ways. To begin with, it provided me with my first earnings. For some reason, there was a sudden demand for tamarind seeds during the war. I would collect the seeds and sell them to a provision store near our house. A day's collection would fetch me the then princely amount of one *anna*!

That was not all. At first, Rameswaram, tucked away in the southern part of the country, was unaffected by the war. Soon, however, India joined in the British war-effort, and war-time measures and economies were instituted. As a result, the train halt at Rameswaram station was suspended. The bundles of newspapers were now tossed out of the moving train, onto the road between Rameswaram and Dhanuskodi. Samsuddin was forced to enlist help, and he chose me to help him move the bundles.

More than fifty years later, I can still feel the thrill and pride I experienced in earning my own money for the first time.

✳ ✳ ✳

It is a well-known fact that both heredity and environment play important roles in moulding an individual. My parents gave me much, as they did to my three brothers and to my sister. We learnt from their honesty and self-discipline, kindness and deep-rooted faith in goodness. I also benefitted from my interaction with Jallaluddin and Samsuddin, whose wisdom was based on intuition rather than instruction. I have no hesitation in saying that whatever creativity I may have displayed later in my life was inspired by their presence in my childhood.

I had three other close friends in my childhood. They were closer to my age, and all of them—Ramanadha Sastry, Aravindan and Sivaprakasan—came from orthodox Hindu Brahmin families. In fact, Ramanadha Sastry was the son of Pakshi Lakshmana Sastry, the high priest of the Rameswaram temple. Later, he took over the priesthood of the Rameswaram temple from his father. Aravindan went into the business of arranging transport for pilgrims and Sivaprakasan became a catering contractor for Southern Railways.

In the epic *Ramayana*, Rameswaram is the site from which Rama is said to have launched his assault on the evil king Ravana. This mention in the epic placed Rameswaram on the Hindu religious map. During the annual *Shri Sita Rama Kalyanam* ceremony held to commemorate this occasion, our family used to arrange the boats that carried the idols from the temple to the marriage site, situated in the middle of the Rama Tirtha pond. As such, events from both the *Ramayana* and the life of Prophet Muhammad formed the bedtime stories my mother and grandmother would tell us. We grew up imbibing both cultures and religions.

However, the small society of Rameswaram was highly stratified and quite rigid about the segregation of different social groups. When I was in the fifth standard, we had a new teacher at the

Rameswaram Elementary School. At the time, I used to wear a cap which marked me as a Muslim. I always sat in the front row next to Ramanadha Sastry, who wore the sacred thread of the Brahmins. The new teacher could not tolerate a Hindu priest's son sitting with a Muslim boy, and I was asked to go and sit right at the back of the class, in accordance with my 'social ranking', as the teacher saw it. I felt very sad, and so did Ramanadha Sastry.

After school, we told our parents about the incident. Lakshmana Sastry summoned the teacher, and in our presence told him, "You must not spread the poison of social inequality and communal intolerance in the minds of innocent children."

Like Lakshmana Sastry, my science teacher Sivasubramania Iyer was a person with a broad social outlook. An orthodox Brahmin in his upbringing, he was something of a rebel at heart. He often said to me, "Kalam, you must develop your skills so that you can compete with the highly educated people in big cities."

One day, he invited me home for a meal. His wife, a very conservative lady, was horrified at the idea of a Muslim boy being invited to dine in her ritually pure kitchen. She refused to serve me. Sivasubramania Iyer served me himself and sat down beside me to eat while his wife watched us from behind the kitchen door. I wondered if she thought that the way I ate rice, drank water or cleaned the floor after the meal was any different from the ways of the high-caste Hindus who were allowed into her kitchen.

When I was leaving his house, Sivasubramania Iyer invited me to join him for a meal again the next weekend. I was hesitant, but when I did visit his house the next week, Sivasubramania Iyer's wife invited me inside her kitchen and served me food with her own hands.

✳ ✳ ✳

Around this time, Germany and Japan surrendered before the collective might of the Allied forces and World War II was over. Freedom from British rule seemed imminent for Indians. Mahatma Gandhi declared that 'Indians would build their own India.' The whole country was filled with an optimism, the likes of which had never been seen before. The optimism affected me too and I asked my father if I could leave Rameswaram to study in Ramanathapuram, a much larger town.

My father said, "Abdul! Going away is a part of growing up. Our love will not bind you nor will our needs hold you."

Samsuddin and Ahmed Jallaluddin travelled with me to Ramanathapuram to enrol me in Schwartz High School, and to arrange for my boarding there.

I did not take to the new setting at first. Ramanathapuram was a thriving town of fifty thousand people, but it lacked the harmony of Rameswaram. I missed my home and grabbed every opportunity to visit Rameswaram. The pull of educational opportunities at Ramanathapuram was not strong enough to cancel the attraction of *poli*, a south Indian sweet that my mother often made.

Despite these frequent bouts of homesickness, I was determined to settle down in the new environment because I knew my father had great hopes for my success. My father visualised me as a collector-in-the-making and I thought it my duty to realise my father's dream. Jallaluddin had once spoken to me about the power of positive thinking and I often recalled his words when I felt dejected. I tried hard to do as he said. He told me I had to strive to control my thoughts and, through these, to influence my destiny. Ironically, that destiny did not lead me back to Rameswaram, but rather, swept me away from the home of my childhood.

3.   EDUCATION PROVIDES A SOLID FOUNDATION

I took some time to settle down at Schwartz High School, but when I did I was back to being an enthusiastic fifteen-year-old student. I also grew to realise that the desire to learn was very important. One of my teachers there, Iyadurai Solomon, was an ideal guide. He was warm and open-minded, and he made his students feel comfortable in class. During my stay at Ramanathapuram, he became my mentor. He made me realise, among other things, that one could exercise enormous influence over the events of one's own life.

Iyadurai Solomon taught me that in order to make anything happen, I must desire it intensely. I must also be completely certain that it would happen. I have grown to realise that this kind of conviction is not only a strong motivating force, but it also does make things happen.

I can illustrate this with an example from my own life. I was always fascinated by the mysteries contained in the skies. Equally fascinating was the flight of birds. A simple boy, from a remote part of the country, I was convinced that, one day, I too would fly. In later years, I became the first child from Rameswaram to fly.

Iyadurai Solomon was a great teacher because he instilled in children a sense of their own worth. He raised my self-esteem and convinced me, a child of parents who had not had the benefits of a good education, that I too could aspire to become whatever I wished. "With faith, you can change your destiny," he said.

By the time I completed my education at Schwartz, I was confident and determined to succeed. The decision to study further was taken without a second thought. The nearest college was St. Joseph's at Tiruchchirappalli, a town more easily identified by its shortened name, Trichy.

✳ ✳ ✳

In 1950, I arrived at St. Joseph's College to study for the Intermediate examination. I was not a bright student in terms of examination grades but, thanks to my friends back in Rameswaram, I had acquired a practical bent of mind.

My good fortune with teachers continued at St. Joseph's College. Rev. Father TN Sequeira taught us English and was also our hostel warden. We were about a hundred boys living in the three-storeyed hostel building and Father Sequeira's energy and patience were amazing. He was very considerate, taking care of the smallest requirements of his students.

I stayed on the St. Joseph's campus for four years. I had two roommates—one, an orthodox Iyengar Brahmin from Srirangam, and the other, a Syrian Christian from Kerala. The three of us had a wonderful time together. I vividly remember an incident from those days. We had invited our Catholic Rector, Rev. Father Kalathil, for lunch one Sunday. The menu included choice preparations from our diverse backgrounds. The result was rather unexpected, and the Rector was lavish in his praise. We enjoyed every moment with Father Kalathil, who participated in our unsophisticated conversation with enthusiasm.

When I was in my final year at St. Joseph's, I acquired a taste for English literature and Philosophy. I began to read the great classics—Tolstoy, Scott and Hardy were special favourites even though it was not easy to relate to their exotic setting. It was also around this time that I developed a keen interest in Physics.

✳ ✳ ✳

After my Intermediate exam, I joined the B.Sc. course at St. Joseph's College. At the time, I had no knowledge of other avenues of higher education or of professional courses. It was only after I passed out of college that I realised that Physics, though fascinating, was not my subject. I needed to take up Engineering to realise my dreams—and should have done this straight after the Intermediate exam. Better late than never, I decided. I applied for admission at the Madras Institute of Technology (MIT), at that time and even now, among the best places for technical education in India.

I managed to get on the list of selected candidates, but admission to the prestigious institution was an expensive affair. Around a thousand rupees were required; a huge amount in those days, and a sum my father could not spare. Zohara mortgaged her gold bangles and chain in order to help me out. I was deeply touched by her determination to see me educated. I promised myself that I would redeem her bangles as soon as possible, with my own earnings. The only way to do that was to study hard and get a scholarship. I went at my studies, determined to do well.

* * *

In the years I spent ay MIT, my curiosity was aroused by two de-commissioned aircraft which were kept on display to demonstrate the various subsystems of flying machines. I felt a strange attraction towards them, and would sit near them long after the other students had gone back to the hostel. I had always admired the human will to fly. After completing my first year, when I had to opt for a specific branch, I almost spontaneously chose Aeronautical Engineering. My goal was very clear now— I was going to fly aircraft.

In the course of my education at MIT, three teachers shaped my thinking. Their instruction formed the foundation on which I later built my professional career. Professors Sponder, KAV Pandalai and Narasingha Rao were distinct personalities, different in many ways but sharing a common trait—the capacity to feed their students' intellectual hunger with brilliance and untiring zeal.

Prof. Sponder taught me technical aerodynamics. He was an Austrian with immense practical experience in Aeronautical Engineering. During World War II, he had been imprisoned in a concentration camp by the Nazis. Since that horrific experience, he had developed a strong aversion to all Germans, even those who had not supported the Nazi party during the war.

Incidentally, a German, Prof. Walter Repenthin, headed the Aeronautics Department. Another well-known professor in the department was Dr. Kurt Tank, a distinguished aeronautical engineer who had designed the German *FockeWulf FW 190*, a single-seater fighter plane and an outstanding combat aircraft of World War II. Dr. Tank later joined Hindustan Aeronautics Limited (HAL) in Bangalore and designed India's first jet fighter, the *HF-24 Marut*.

Prof. Sponder learned to work with his German colleagues, despite his differences. He was always calm, energetic and in control of himself. He kept abreast of the latest technologies and expected his students to do the same.

I consulted him when I first thought of opting for Aeronautical Engineering. He told me that one should never worry about one's foundations, but have a sufficient amount of aptitude and passion for one's chosen field of study. The trouble with many students, Prof. Sponder observed, was not necessarily a lack of educational opportunities or industrial infrastructure—the trouble was in their failure to choose their field of study with sufficient care.

Prof. Pandalai taught aero-structure design and analysis. He was a friendly and enthusiastic teacher, who brought a fresh approach to every teaching course. It was Prof. Pandalai who unlocked the secrets of structural engineering to us. I believe that everyone who has been taught by Prof. Pandalai will agree that he was a man of great intellectual integrity and scholarship—with no trace of arrogance. His students were free to disagree with him in classroom discussions.

Prof. Narasingha Rao was a mathematician, who taught us theoretical aerodynamics. After attending his classes, I began to prefer mathematical physics to any other subject. In later years, I have often been told I carry a 'surgical knife' to aeronautical design reviews. If it had not been for Prof. Rao's persistent advice on how to prove equations in aerodynamics, I would not have acquired this skill.

Aeronautics is a fascinating subject. Slowly, an amalgamation of information took place in my mind. I began to understand the differences in structure in the various types of aircraft. My favourite professors, all of them authorities in their different fields, helped me to acquire this composite knowledge.

✳ ✳ ✳

My third and final year at MIT was a year of transition. A new wave of thought—political and industrial—swept through the country in those years. The popular view in those days was that a belief in scientific methods was the only valid approach to knowledge. If so, I wondered, what about spiritual association? I had been brought up with deeply religious values, where true realisation lay beyond the material world—in a wholly spiritual realm. I had been taught from my early childhood that knowledge could be obtained only through the inner experience. I wondered about these and other ethical issues, attempting to sort out questions of science and my own spiritual interests.

Meanwhile, when I had finished my course work, I was assigned a project to design a low-level attack aircraft along with four other students. I was put in charge of drawing its aerodynamic design and my team-mates distributed the other tasks among themselves. Prof. Srinivasan—then director of MIT—reviewed my work and declared it disappointing. I offered a dozen excuses for the substandard work, but none of them impressed Prof. Srinivasan.

I finally pleaded for a month's time to complete the task. The professor looked at me for some time and said, "Today is Friday afternoon. I can give you three days' time. If I don't get the configuration drawing by Monday morning, your scholarship will be revoked."

I was dumbstruck. The scholarship was my lifeline! I had to finish the task immediately. That whole night, I sat at the drawing board, skipping dinner. I took an hour's break to freshen up and eat a little food the next morning. On Sunday, I was very near completion when I heard someone enter my room. It was Prof. Srinivasan on his way back from the club, still in his tennis clothes. He had dropped in to see my progress.

He examined my work, after which he patted my back affectionately, saying, "I knew I was putting you under great pressure with that impossible deadline. And honestly, I never expected you to perform so well!"

I also enjoyed extra-curricular work. While in MIT, I participated in an essay-writing competition organised by the Tamil Sangam (a literary society). I wrote an article, 'Let us make our own aircraft', in Tamil. The article evoked much interest and I even won the competition. Tamil is my mother tongue and a language that has hugely influenced me.

The most cherished memory from college, however, is related to Prof. Sponder. At the end of the final year, we were posing for a class photograph, which was part of the farewell ritual. All the graduating students had lined up in three rows, with the professors seated in the front. Suddenly, Prof. Sponder got up and looked for me. I was standing in the third row.

"Come and sit with me in the front," he said. "You are my best student. I believe your hard work will help you heap honour on your teachers."

I was taken aback; embarrassed by the praise, but honoured by the recognition. I moved forward slowly and sat with Prof. Sponder for the photograph.

---

4.   Preparing to Start a Career

From MIT, I went as a trainee to Hindustan Aeronautics Limited (HAL) at Bangalore, where I worked on engine overhauling as part of a team. It was hands-on work and very educative; I was able to apply much of what I had learned earlier in theory. When a principle learnt in the classroom is borne out by practical experience, it creates a strange sense of excitement—like unexpectedly running into an old friend among a crowd of strangers.

I found the HAL technicians very intriguing. They had neither studied in major universities, nor were they just following the orders that their engineer-in-charge was putting forward. They had been working with this technology for years and seemed to have developed an intuitive feel for the work.

Soon after, two different opportunities for employment—both close to my long-standing dream of flying—came up when I left HAL as a graduate aeronautical engineer. One was a career in the Indian Air Force (IAF), the other, a job at the Directorate of

Technical Development and Production or DTD&P (Air), of the Ministry of Defence. I applied for both. I was called for interviews at both places almost simultaneously. I was asked to come to Dehradun by the air force recruitment authorities and to New Delhi by DTD&P (Air).

The boy from the Coromandel coast travelled to the north for the first time, to a destination more than 2,000 km away. It was to be my first encounter with the vastness of my country.

Through the window of the train compartment, I watched the countryside slip past. From a distance, the men and women working in the paddy fields seemed to be part of a painting. I sat glued to the window. Almost everywhere, people were engaged in some activity which had a rhythm in it—men driving cattle, women fetching water—all things that they have done for centuries. Occasionally, a child would appear and wave at the train as it passed.

It is astonishing how the landscape changes as one travels across India; it could almost be like travelling through a different country. To bring me to Delhi, my train had to cross the geographical barriers of the Narmada, Tapti, Mahanadi, Godavari and Krishna rivers. To me, the journey was also a tribute to the power of science and the human capacity to invent.

I halted a week in Delhi, the city of the great Sufi saint, Hazrat Nizamuddin. I did well in the interview at DTD&P (Air). The questions were routine, and did not challenge my knowledge of the subject. I was quite confident that I had done well. Then, I proceeded to Dehradun for my interview at the Air Force Selection Board where the story was somewhat different.

At the Selection Board, the emphasis was on personality, physical fitness and the ability to speak well. I was excited but nervous, determined but anxious, confident but tense.

I only managed to finish ninth in the batch of 25 candidates, from which eight officers were to be selected for the IAF.

I was disappointed. It took some time for me to comprehend that an opportunity to join the air force had just slipped through my fingers. I dragged myself out of the Selection Board knowing that the days ahead would be difficult. I had to overcome my disappointment somehow. I also had to prepare a new plan of action, since the career of my choice now seemed to be out of reach. I decided to go on a journey to soothe my mind. Rishikesh, with its peaceful atmosphere, seemed to me an ideal place and I trekked to the pilgrimage spot with a lot on my mind.

※　※　※

I walked to the Sivananda Ashram in Rishikesh. There, I met Swami Sivananda, who seemed to me to be the image of the Buddha. He had an olive complexion and black, piercing eyes, and he was dressed in a white dhoti and wooden sandals. I was struck by his irresistible smile and gracious manner. I introduced myself to him. Before I could speak any further, he asked me why I was sorrowful. He offered me no explanation of how he knew I was sad, and I did not ask.

I told him of my unsuccessful attempt to join the IAF and my long-cherished desire to fly. He comforted me with these powerful words, "Accept your destiny and go ahead with your life. Perhaps you are not destined to become a pilot. What you are destined to become is not revealed as yet, but it is pre-determined. Forget this failure. Think of it as a step that will lead you to your pre-destined path."

When the student is ready, the teacher will appear. The truth of this statement hit me with full force. Here was a teacher who had shown me the way when I needed help most. He re-affirmed what my father had taught me—that learning to cope with setbacks, disappointments and thwarted hopes is a part of life.

I returned to Delhi and enquired at DTD&P (Air) about the outcome of my interview. In response, I was handed my appointment letter. I joined the next day as senior scientific assistant on a basic salary of Rs. 250 per month.

If this was to be my destiny, I thought, let it be so. No more did I feel bitterness or resentment at my failure to enter the IAF. I also realised that although I was not flying aeroplanes, I was helping to make them airworthy!

---

5.   WORK BEGINS IN EARNEST

All this was in 1958. At the Directorate, I was posted at the Technical Centre (Civil Aviation). During my first year, I carried out a design assignment on supersonic target aircraft with the help of the officer-in-charge, R Varadharajan. The design won a word of praise from the director, Dr. Neelakantan. Soon, I was sent to the Aircraft and Armament Testing Unit (A&ATU) at Kanpur to gain actual experience and practice in aircraft maintenance. The *Gnat Mark II* aircraft was being assessed, and I was to work on it.

It was my first experience of living in an industrial town. Even in those days, Kanpur was heavily populated. The cold weather, crowds, noise and smoke were in total contrast to what I was used to in Rameswaram. I was particularly irritated by the cook's constant dependence on potatoes, from breakfast to dinner!

To me, it also seemed that a feeling of loneliness pervaded the city. Many of the inhabitants had come from their villages looking for jobs in the factories, leaving behind the places they had grown up in and were familiar with. They seemed to belong as little as I did.

On my return to Delhi, I was informed that the design of a new type of target had been taken up at DTD&P (Air) and that I had been included in the design team. I completed this task with the other team members. Then, I undertook a preliminary design study on human centrifuge. I later carried out the design and development of a vertical take-off and landing platform.

Three years passed. Then, the Aeronautical Development Establishment (ADE) was born in Bangalore, and I was posted to the new establishment. In the first year, the workload at ADE was quite light. In fact, I had to create work for myself till the tempo gradually built up.

Soon, based on my preliminary studies, a project team was formed to design and develop an indigenous hovercraft prototype, a ground equipment machine (GEM). It was a small working group of four persons, with me to lead the team. We were given three years to launch the engineering model.

The project was, by any standards, bigger than all our capabilities put together. None of us had any real experience in building a machine, let alone a flying machine. There were no designs or standard parts available. All we knew was that we had to make a successful, heavier-than-air, flying machine. We tried to read all that we could find on hovercrafts, but there was not much material available. We tried to consult people knowledgeable in this area, but could find none.

One day, I decided to go ahead with the limited information and resources available. After spending a few months on the drawing board, we moved straight on to the actual model. Part by part, subsystem by subsystem, stage by stage, things started moving. This endeavour to produce a wingless, light, swift machine opened the windows of my mind.

There is always the danger that a person with a background such as mine—small town, middle class, with parents who had had a limited education—would shrink from too much responsibility, content to have come so far, waiting for a stroke of fate to take the next big step. I always knew that I, and not just fate, would have to create my own opportunities.

At that time VK Krishna Menon was the defence minister of India. He was keenly interested in the progress of our small project. He saw it as a stepping stone to India producing defence equipment within the country. Whenever he was in Bangalore, he always found some time to check on our progress. His confidence set the tone for our enthusiasm.

But not everyone accepted Krishna Menon's opinion of the GEM. Our experiments with the available parts and components did not delight my senior colleagues. Many called us a group of eccentric inventors in pursuit of an impossible dream. I was a particularly inviting target as I was regarded as yet another country lad with no hold on reality. But, this weight of opinion against us fired our ever-optimistic minds.

When the project was about a year old, the defence minister made one of his routine visits to ADE. I escorted him into our assembly shop. Inside, on a table, lay the GEM. The model was the culmination of one year's untiring efforts to develop a practical hovercraft for battlefield applications. The minister fired one question after another at me, determined to ensure that the prototype would go into test flight within the coming year.

The hovercraft was christened *Nandi*, after the impressive white bull who acts as Shiva's vehicle. For a prototype, its form, fit and finish were rudimentary. But, it went beyond our expectations, given the basic equipment we possessed. I told my colleagues, "This flying machine has been constructed by engineers of ability.

Don't form your opinions based on its looks. It is not made to be looked at, but to fly with."

Later, Defence Minister VK Krishna Menon took a ride in *Nandi* with me at the helm, overruling all statements of concern for his safety. A group captain, who had logged in many thousands of flying hours, offered to fly the machine. He gestured to me to move out of the machine, signalling the danger the minister was putting himself in by flying with an inexperienced civilian pilot like myself. I knew the machine that I had created, and was sure that I was competent enough to fly it. I shook my head at the group captain. Observing this wordless communication, the minister dismissed the insulting suggestion of the group captain with a laugh and signalled to me to start the machine.

It was a smooth ride and the minister said to me, "You have demonstrated that the basic problems of hovercraft development are now solved. You must develop a more powerful prime mover and call me for a second ride."

✳ ✳ ✳

We completed the project ahead of schedule; creating a successful working hovercraft. Dr. OP Mediratta, director of ADE, was visibly pleased with the achievement. But, by this time, VK Krishna Menon was out of office and could not take his promised second ride. In the new government, not many people shared his dream. The project was mired in controversies and was finally shelved. Even today, we import hovercrafts, relying on outside technology.

The setback in the hovercraft project was a new experience for me. I had put my heart and soul into *Nandi*. The fact that it would not be used practically went beyond my comprehension. I was disappointed and disillusioned. So far, I had believed that the sky was the limit, but it now appeared that the limits were much closer. There are boundaries that dictate life—you can only lift so much weight; you can only learn so fast; you can only work so hard; you can only go so far!

In this period of confusion and uncertainty, memories from my childhood came back to me. Pakshi Lakshmana Sastry used to say, "Seek the truth, and the truth shall set you free." And the Bible says, "Ask and you shall receive." What I desired did not happen immediately, but it happened nevertheless.

One day, Dr. Mediratta called me to inquire about the state of our hovercraft. When told that it was in perfect condition to be flown, he asked me to organise a demonstration for an important visitor the next day. No VIP was scheduled to visit the laboratory during the next week, as far as I knew. However, I communicated Dr. Mediratta's instructions to my colleagues and we felt a new surge of hope.

---

6.   FROM HOVERCRAFT TO ROCKETS

The next day Dr. Mediratta brought a visitor to our hovercraft—a tall, handsome, bearded man. He asked me several questions about the machine. I was immediately struck by his clear thinking.

"Can you give me a ride in the machine?" he enquired after a while. His request filled me with joy—finally, here was someone who was interested in our work!

We took a ten-minute ride in the hovercraft, a few centimetres above the ground. We were not flying, but were definitely floating in the air. The visitor asked me a few questions about myself, thanked me for the ride and departed.

That man was Prof. MGK Menon, director of the Tata Institute of Fundamental Research (TIFR). After a week, I received a call from the Indian Committee for Space Research (INCOSPAR), to attend an interview for the post of a rocket engineer. All I knew about INCOSPAR at that time was that it was formed out of the TIFR talent pool at Bombay (now Mumbai) to organise space research in India.

I went to Bombay to attend the interview, unsure about the type of questions I would have to face. I reminded myself that the best way to win was to not feel that desperate need to win. The best performances are accomplished when you are relaxed and free of doubt. I decided to take things as they came. It was easy for me to do this because neither Prof. Menon's visit nor the call for an interview had been of my making.

I was interviewed by Prof. Vikram Sarabhai along with Prof. Menon and Mr. Saraf, then deputy secretary of the Atomic Energy Commission. As I entered the room, I sensed their warmth and friendliness. There was none of the arrogance or the patronising attitude that interviewers usually display when talking to a young and vulnerable candidate.

I was also immediately struck by Prof. Sarabhai. His questions did not probe my knowledge or skills; they were instead an exploration of the possibilities I saw within myself. He was looking at me as if in reference to a larger whole. The entire encounter seemed to me a total moment of truth, in which my dream was enveloped by the larger dream of a bigger person.

I was advised to stay back for a couple of days. However, the next evening I was told that I was to be absorbed as a rocket engineer at INCOSPAR. This was a breakthrough a young man like myself could only have dreamed of.

✳ ✳ ✳

My work at INCOSPAR commenced with a familiarisation course at the TIFR computer centre. The atmosphere here was remarkably different from that at DTD&P (Air). Labels mattered very little. There was no need for anyone to justify his or her position, or to be at the receiving end of another's hostility.

Some time in the later half of 1962, INCOSPAR took the decision to set up its Equatorial Rocket Launching Station at Thumba, a sleepy fishing village near Trivandrum (now Thiruvananthapuram) in Kerala. Dr. Chitnis of the Physical Research Laboratory, Ahmedabad had spotted it as a suitable location—it was very close to the earth's magnetic equator. This was the beginning of modern rocket-based research in India; unassuming and with little fanfare.

The site selected at Thumba lay between the railway line and the west coast, covering a distance of about two and a half kilometres and measuring about 600 acres. Within this area stood a large church, the land of which had to be acquired to build the station. Acquiring private land is always a difficult and slow process, especially in densely populated places like Kerala. In addition, there was the delicate matter of acquiring a site of religious significance. The collector of Trivandrum, K Madhavan Nair, executed this task tactfully, with the co-operation of the Right Rev. Dr. Dereira, who was the bishop of Trivandrum in1962.

Soon RD John, the executive engineer of the Central Public Works Department (CPWD), had transformed the entire area. The St. Mary Magdalene church housed the first office of the Thumba Space Centre. The prayer room was my first laboratory; the bishop's room was my design and drawing office. (To this day, the church is maintained as it was and, at present, houses the Indian Space Museum.)

Very soon after this, I was asked to attend a six-month training programme on sounding rocket launching techniques at the National Aeronautics and Space Administration (NASA) work centres in the USA.

I took some time off to visit Rameswaram before the journey. My father was very pleased to learn about the opportunity that had come my way. He took me to the mosque and organised a special namaaz.

Jallaluddin and Samsuddin came to see me off at Bombay airport. It was their first exposure to a metropolis like Bombay, just as I myself was about to be introduced to a megapolis like New York. When Jallaluddin said, "Azad, we have always loved and believed in you. We shall always be proud of you," the intensity and purity of their faith in my capabilities broke my defences, and tears welled up in my eyes.

❋ ❋ ❋

I joined work at NASA's research centre in Virginia. This is primarily a centre for research and development in advanced aerospace technology. From there, I went to Maryland, to the Goddard Space Flight Centre.

I was impressed by the organisational structure of these institutions in the US. They appeared to me to be made up of people who met their problems head-on. They also did not seem to suffer from false pride, which was such a big barrier to effective growth in several Indian institutions.

It brought to mind an incident my mother had told me from the Bible. After God created man, the angels were asked to prostrate themselves before Adam. Everybody prostrated themselves except Satan, who refused.

"Why do you not prostrate yourself?" asked God in anger.

"You created me of fire and Adam of clay," responded Satan scornfully. "Does not that make me nobler?"

In answer he received thunderous censure from God, "Be gone! This is no place in paradise for your contemptuous pride."

Such 'contemptuous pride' is widespread in many organisations. It stops managers from listening to their subordinates and people down the line. I have always thought that one cannot expect people to deliver results if you humiliate them; nor can you expect them to be creative if you don't respect their ability. The line between firmness and harshness, between strong leadership and bullying, between discipline and vindictiveness is very fine, but it has to be drawn.

Dealing with problems is often a painful process, requiring hard work, so we tend to put things off. Actually, learning to solve problems can help us distinguish between success and failure. They make us rely on our innate courage and wisdom.

Towards the end of my visit, I went to the east coast of Virginia, where the sounding rocket programme undertaken by NASA was situated. The reception lobby there had on display a painting— it was not an unusual painting to have in such a centre, for it depicted a battle scene, with a few rockets flying in the background. What caught my attention was that the soldiers shown launching the rockets were not white-skinned; they were dark-skinned people with features usually seen in people from south India.

One day, driven by my curiosity, I examined the painting closely. It turned out to be the army of Tipu Sultan fighting the British East India Company towards the end of the eighteenth century. It struck me that, here, on the other side of the planet, the earliest rockets used in warfare were celebrated, as was the foresight of the Indian ruler who first used them. But, in our own country, this fact is little known or appreciated.

✳ ✳ ✳

Soon after I returned from NASA, India's first rocket launch took place, on 21 November 1963. It was a sounding rocket, called *Nike-Apache*, and had been made at NASA. The rocket was assembled in the church building at Thumba. The only equipment available to transport the rocket to the launch pad was a truck and a manually operated hydraulic crane.

The launch was not without a few tense moments. When the rocket was lifted by the crane and was about to be placed on the launcher, it started tilting, indicating a leak in the hydraulic system of the crane. As the launch time of 1800 hrs was approaching, there was no time to repair the crane. Fortunately, the leak was not large and we managed to lift the rocket, using our collective muscle power, and finally placed it on the launcher.

In the maiden *Nike-Apache* launch, I was in charge of rocket integration and safety. Two of my colleagues who played a very active and crucial role in this launch were D Easwardas and R Aravamudan. Easwardas undertook the rocket assembly and arranged the launch. Aravamudan, whom we called Dan, was in charge of radar, telemetry and ground support.

To our joy, the launch was smooth and problem-free and we obtained excellent flight data. All of us felt a sense of pride and accomplishment.

---

7.   ADDING MOMENTUM TO SPACE RESEARCH

The Thumba Equatorial Rocket Launch Station (TERLS) was further developed, in active collaboration with France, the USA and the USSR. It was to be the hub of India's integrated national space programme, with indigenously developed equipment for the manufacture of rockets and launch facilities.

The real journey of the Indian space programme, however, began with the *Rohini* sounding rocket (RSR) programme. This programme was responsible for the development and fabrication of sounding rockets and their associated on-board systems for scientific investigations in India. Under the RSR programme, a family of operational sounding rockets was developed. These rockets had wide ranging capabilities, and to date, several hundred such rockets have been launched for various scientific and technological studies.

The development of these rockets made India capable of producing fully indigenous sounding rockets, as well as their very high-performance solid propellants. The development of Indian rockets in the twentieth century can be seen as a revival of the eighteenth-century vision of Tipu Sultan.

When Tipu Sultan was killed, the British forces captured more than 700 rockets and the subsystems of 900 rockets. These rockets were taken to England and subjected by the British to what we call 'reverse engineering' today—there were no strict patent regimes then!

With the death of Tipu, Indian rocketry came to a standstill—to be revived 150 years later in an independent India.

In that time, rocket technology had made great strides abroad. Konstantin Tsiolkovsky in Russia (1903), Robert Goddard in USA (1914) and Hermann Oberth in Germany (1923) gave rocketry new dimensions. During World War II, Wernher von Braun's team in Nazi Germany produced the effective *V-2* short-range ballistic missiles. After the war, both the USA and the USSR captured their share of German rocket engineers. With this began their deadly Arms Race which was to last for decades.

❊   ❊   ❊

Rocketry was reborn in India thanks to the technological vision of Prime Minister Jawaharlal Nehru. Prof. Vikram Sarabhai took on the challenge of giving physical dimensions to this dream. Very many individuals questioned the relevance of space activities in a newly independent nation; one which was finding it difficult to feed its huge population. But, neither Nehru nor Sarabhai had any such doubts. Their vision was very clear—if India was to play a meaningful role in the community of nations, she must be second to none in the application of advanced technologies.

Prof. Sarabhai was always keen on trying novel ideas and he liked to rope in young people to do this. He had the wisdom and judgement to realise not only if something was well done, but also when it was time to stop. In my opinion, he was an innovator.

This was precisely the situation at INCOSPAR in the early sixties. We were a group of young and inexperienced, but energetic and enthusiastic persons who had been given the task of shaping the Indian spirit of self-reliance in the field of science and technology in general, and of space research in particular. Our biggest qualifications at INCOSPAR were not our degrees and training, but Prof. Sarabhai's faith in our capabilities. It was a great example of leadership by trust.

Prof. Sarabhai's optimism was highly contagious. The very news of his coming to Thumba would electrify the people, and all laboratories, workshops and design offices would hum with unceasing activity. People would work around the clock in their enthusiasm to show Prof. Sarabhai something new, something that had not been done before in our country—be it a new design, a new method of fabrication, or even an out-of-the-ordinary administrative procedure.

Prof. Sarabhai believed in an open and free exchange of views. Perhaps he was aware that though a particular goal might be clear to him, his team members might resist working towards a goal that they could not envision. He felt that without collective understanding of a problem, effective leadership was impossible in a team. He once told me, "My job is to make decisions; but it is equally important to see that these decisions are accepted by my team members."

In fact, Prof. Sarabhai took a series of decisions that were to become the life-mission of many scientists in India. He wanted to create new frontiers in the field of science and technology in India. After the successful launch of *Nike-Apache*, he chose to share with us his dream of an Indian satellite launch vehicle (SLV).

His decision to make our own SLVs and our own satellites—that too simultaneously, in a multi-dimensional fashion—was remarkable. He first discussed the matter threadbare with scientists working in different organisations and at different locations. I often say that the most significant achievement at that time was to establish and maintain nationwide trust in the plan.

✳ ✳ ✳

Perhaps realising that I preferred to persuade people to do as they were told rather than use authority, Prof. Sarabhai assigned to me the task of providing interface support to payload scientists. Almost all physical laboratories in India were involved in the sounding rocket programme—each having its own mission, its own objective and its own payload. We had x-ray payloads to look at stars; payloads to analyse the gas composition of the upper atmosphere; sodium payloads to find out wind conditions, its direction and velocity; and ionospheric payloads to explore the different layers of the atmosphere.

I not only had to interact with scientists from TIFR, the National Physical Laboratory (NPL), and Physical Research Laboratory (PRL), but also with payload scientists from the USA, the USSR, France, West Germany and Japan.

I often read Khalil Gibran, and always find his words full of wisdom. "Bread baked without love is a bitter bread, that feeds but half a man's hunger." Those who cannot work with their hearts achieve a hollow, half-hearted success that only breeds bitterness within.

If you are a writer who would secretly prefer to be a lawyer or a doctor, your written words will feed only half the hunger of your readers; if you are a teacher who would rather be working a business, your teaching will meet only half the need for knowledge of your students; if you are a scientist who hates science, your performance will satisfy only half the needs of your mission. It is critical to become emotionally involved with one's work, such that any obstruction to the success of that work fills one with grief.

I have worked with several people whose dedication to work is exemplary. One such was Prof. Oda, who was an x-ray payload scientist from the Institute of Space and Aeronautical Sciences (ISAS), Japan. I remember him as a tiny man with a towering personality and eyes that radiated intelligence. The x-ray payloads he brought would be engineered by my team to fit into the nose cone of the *Rohini.*

One day, when I was working on the integration of Prof. Oda's payload with my timer devices, he insisted on using the timers he had brought from Japan. To me they looked flimsy, but Prof. Oda stuck to his stand that the Indian timers must be replaced by the Japanese ones. I yielded to his suggestion and replaced the timers.

The rocket took off elegantly and attained the intended altitude. Soon, however, the telemetry signal reported mission failure on account of timer malfunction. Prof. Oda was so upset that tears welled up in his eyes. I was stunned by the intensity of Prof. Oda's response. He clearly cared very deeply to see that his work was of consequence.

At TERLS, I was also involved with building subsystems like payload housing and jettisonable nose cones. Working with the nose cones led me, as a natural consequence, into the field of composite materials.

It is interesting to know that the bows found during archaeological excavations reveal that people from the Indian subcontinent used composite bows made of wood, sinew, and horn, as early as the eleventh century—at least 500 years before such bows were made in Medieval Europe. I was so enthused with the versatility of these composite materials that I wanted to know everything about them almost overnight!

✳ ✳ ✳

Slowly, but surely, two Indian rockets were born at Thumba. They were christened *Rohini* and *Menaka*, after the two mythological dancers in the court of Indra. It was also a huge achievement that the Indian payloads no longer needed to be launched by French rockets.

Could this have been done without the atmosphere of trust and commitment which Prof. Sarabhai had created at INCOSPAR? He utilised each person's knowledge and skills, making every member of the staff feel directly involved in problem solving. At the same time, if he found any one of us with an excessive workload, or attempting a task without the required capability or skill, he would reorganise our work activity so as to reduce the pressure on us, and help us to perform better.

By the time the first *Rohini-75* rocket was launched from TERLS on 20 November 1967, almost each one of us had settled into a familiar groove.

8.   Balancing Defence Technology with Space Research

Early next year, Prof. Sarabhai wanted to see me urgently in New Delhi. By now I was accustomed to his unusual working methods and sudden flashes of inspiration. On reaching Delhi, I contacted his secretary for an appointment and was asked to meet him at 3.30 a.m. at Hotel Ashoka. Delhi was a slightly unfamiliar place, with an unfriendly winter climate for someone like me, used to the warm and humid climate of southern India. I decided to wait in the hotel lounge after finishing my dinner.

I looked around the elegant lounge. Somebody had left a book on a nearby sofa. I picked up the book and started browsing through it. It was a popular book related to business management and I was skimming through it, skipping paragraphs and turning pages. Suddenly, my eyes fell on one particular passage. It was a quotation from George Bernard Shaw. I remember the passage clearly.

It said that all reasonable men adapt themselves to the world. Only a few unreasonable ones persist in trying to adapt the world to themselves. All progress in the world depends on these unreasonable men and their new and often revolutionary actions.

I started reading the book. The passage described certain myths woven around industry and business, such as the myth of strategic planning. The author was of the opinion that it is essential for a project manager to learn to live with uncertainty and ambiguity. And that it is a myth that, to win big, one must strive to create perfect conditions for success. This helps one win only on paper, but to invariably lose in the real chaotic world.

It struck me then that this could be true of our space programme. Waiting in a hotel lobby at 1.00 a.m. for an appointment was certainly not reasonable, neither for me nor for Prof. Sarabhai. But then, he was always rather unorthodox in his approach. He was running the country's space research establishment—under-staffed and over-worked—but nevertheless successfully.

Suddenly, I became aware of another man who came and sat down on the sofa opposite mine. He was a well-built person and looked intelligent and refined. Unlike me—always disorderly in my dress—this man wore elegant clothes. And, despite the odd hour, he was alert.

Before I could get back to the book, I was informed that Prof. Sarabhai was ready to receive me. I left the book on the sofa from where I had picked it up. I was surprised when the man sitting on the opposite sofa was also asked to come inside. Who was he?

Even before we sat down, Prof. Sarabhai introduced us to each other. He was Group Captain VS Narayanan from the IAF. Prof. Sarabhai ordered coffee for both of us and unfolded his plan of developing a rocket-assisted take-off system (RATO) for military aircraft. This would help our fighter planes to take off from the short runways in the Himalaya. Hot coffee was served over small talk. As soon as we finished the coffee, Prof. Sarabhai rose and asked us to accompany him to Tilpat Range, on the outskirts of New Delhi.

The Indian Air Force was in dire need of a large number of RATO motors for their *S-22* and *HF-24* aircraft. RATO motors were mounted on aircraft to provide the additional thrust required during take-off for aircraft flying under adverse operating conditions—like partially bombed runways, high altitude airfields, a heavier than prescribed load, or very high temperatures.

✳ ✳ ✳

Two significant developments occurred during the subsequent work on RATO motors. The first was the release of a ten-year profile for space research in the country, prepared by Prof. Sarabhai. It was not just an activity plan, but a theme paper meant for open discussions, to be later transformed into a programme.

The plan mainly centred on the early ideas which had been born at INCOSPAR. It included the utilisation of satellites for television and developmental education, and meteorological observations and remote sensing for the management of natural resources. To this was now added the development and launch of satellite launch vehicles for low earth orbit, and the upgrading and improvement of Indian satellites.

Today, we in India take most of these developments very much for granted, which is testimony to the visionary qualities of Prof. Sarabhai. The active international aid that had been necessary for years was more or less done away with in the new plan and the emphasis was on self-reliance and indigenous technologies. Over and above, there was the dream of an adequate infrastructure that would be capable of supporting research and development (R&D) in a variety of engineering and scientific disciplines.

The second development was the formation of a Missile Panel in the Ministry of Defence. Both Narayanan and I were inducted as members. The idea of making missiles in our own country was exciting, and we spent hours studying the missiles made in various technologically advanced countries.

What is it that distinguishes a sounding rocket from a satellite launch vehicle, and these from a missile? In fact, all three are different kinds of rockets.

Sounding rockets are normally used to probe the near-earth environment, including the upper regions of the atmosphere. While they can carry a variety of scientific payloads to a range of altitudes, they cannot impart the final velocity needed to orbit the payload.

On the other hand, a launch vehicle is designed to inject a technological payload, or satellite, into orbit. The final stage of a launch vehicle provides the necessary velocity for a satellite to enter its orbit. This is a complex operation requiring on-board guidance and control systems.

A missile, though belonging to the same family as these two, is a still more complex system. In addition to the large terminal velocity and on-board guidance and control systems, it must have the capability to home onto its target. When its target is fast-moving and capable of manoeuvering, a missile should also be able to carry out target-tracking functions.

Narayanan was a great admirer of the strong approach of the Russian missile development programme. He also had tremendous enthusiasm for indigenous guided missiles.

The bitter lessons of the two wars (in 1962 against China and 1965 against Pakistan) had left the Indian leadership with little choice in the matter of achieving self-reliance in military hardware and weapon systems. A large number of surface-to-air missiles (SAMs) were obtained from the USSR to guard strategic locations. Narayanan passionately advocated the development of these missiles in our own country.

Right from the day of our pre-dawn visit to the Tilpat Range with Prof. Sarabhai, Narayanan was always busy with the RATO motor. He had arranged everything that was required before being asked. He obtained Rs. 75 lakh as funding for the task, with a further promise that any unforeseen costs would be met.

"I can get you whatever material you need. But you must promise never to ask for extra time!" he said. I often laughed at his impatience.

Defence R&D at that time was heavily dependent on imported equipment. Virtually nothing indigenous was available. Together, we made a long shopping list and drew up an import plan. But this made me unhappy—was there no remedy or alternative? Could a poor country like India afford this kind of development?

One day, while working late in the office—quite a regular practice after I took up the RATO project—I spotted a young colleague, Jaya Chandra Babu, who had joined us a few months ago. I called him into my office and discussed these problems with him.

"Do you have any suggestions?" I asked him. Babu was silent for a while, and then asked for one day's time to answer my question.

The next evening, Babu's face was beaming with promise. "We can do it, sir! The RATO system can be made without importing equipment."

He asked for relaxations such as financial approval by a single person instead of an entire hierarchy, air travel for all people on work, lifting of goods by air-cargo, sub-contracting to the private sector, placement of orders on the basis of technical competence, and smooth and quick accounting procedures. All of these would streamline our working.

These demands were unheard of in government establishments, which are bureaucratic and very conservative. Yet I could see the soundness of his proposition. The RATO project was new and there was nothing wrong if it could be worked with a new set of rules. I weighed all the pros and cons and finally presented them to Prof. Sarabhai. He approved the proposals without a second thought, convinced of its merits.

Babu had highlighted the importance of clever business practices in developmental work. Sadly, he did not remain with us for long, and left for greener pastures in Nigeria. I can never forget Babu's common sense in financial matters.

9. DREAMING OF SATELLITES

In February 1969, Prime Minister Indira Gandhi visited Thumba to dedicate TERLS to the International Space Science Community. On this occasion, she commissioned the country's first filament winding machine in our laboratory. This event brought my team—which included CR Satya, PN Subramanian and MN Satyanarayana—great satisfaction.

In 1969, Prof. Sarabhai also decided to go full-steam ahead in building and launching our own satellites indigenously. He took part in an aerial survey of the east coast for a possible site. He concentrated on the east coast so that the launch vehicle could take full advantage of the earth's west-to-east rotation. He finally selected Sriharikota island, a hundred kilometres north of Madras (now Chennai). Thus the SHAR Rocket Launch Station was born. The crescent-shaped island has a maximum width of eight kilometres and lies alongside the coastline. In area, it is as big as Madras city.

In 1968, we had formed the Indian Rocket Society. Soon after, INCOSPAR was reconstituted as an advisory body under the Indian National Science Academy (INSA) and the Indian Space Research Organisation (ISRO) was created under the Department of Atomic Energy (DAE) to conduct space research in the country.

By this time, Prof. Sarabhai had already hand-picked a team to give form to his dream of an Indian SLV. It came to be known as SLV-3. I consider myself fortunate to have been chosen to be a project leader. Prof. Sarabhai also gave me the additional responsibility of designing the fourth stage of SLV-3.

Dr. VR Gowarikar, MR Kurup and AE Muthunayagam were given the tasks of designing the other three stages.

As a project manager, I have always considered that the price of perfection is much too high, and therefore allowed mistakes as a part of the learning process. I prefer a dash of daring and persistence to perfection. I have always supported learning on the part of my team members, whether their attempts are successful or unsuccessful.

I laid the foundation for Stage IV on two rocks. Although I provided access to all the information that my co-workers in Stage IV needed, I found I could not spend enough time to be truly helpful as a source of support. I used to wonder if there was something wrong with the way in which I managed my time.

At this stage, Prof. Sarabhai brought a French visitor to our work centre. This gentleman was Dr. Curien, president of CNES (Centre Nationale de Etudes Spatiales), our counterpart in France. They were then developing the *Diamont* launch vehicles.

Dr. Curien was a thorough professional. Together, they helped me set a target, discussed the means by which I could reach it, and also cautioned me about the possibilities of failure. This helped me get a better awareness of Stage IV problems.

Dr. Curien was so impressed by our planned effort that he inquired if we could also create the *Diamont's* fourth stage. Prof. Sarabhai smiled at the suggestion. As a matter of fact, the *Diamont* and SLV-3 airframes were incompatible, and some major changes were required.

We began to work on the *Diamont's* fourth stage simultaneously. I gave handwritten notes to colleagues on engineering and design, requesting definite action within five or ten days. I also made it a point to have the team meet at least once every week. Though it took up time and energy, I considered it essential. This method worked wonderfully. Dr. Curien testified that we had achieved in a year's time what our counterparts in Europe could barely manage in three years!

How good is a leader? As good as the commitment and participation received from her or his team! Getting the team together to share whatever little development had been achieved— results, experiences, small successes and the like—seemed to me worth putting all my energy and time into. The slight loss of time was a very small price to pay for that commitment and sense of teamwork. Within my own small group of people I found leaders, and learned that leaders exist at every level. This was another important lesson.

I used to observe my own colleagues carefully to see if they had the willingness to experiment constantly. I also started listening to anyone who showed the slightest promise. We continued to work towards modifying SLV-3's Stage IV design to suit the *Diamont* airframe. After two years of effort, when we were about to deliver it to CNES, the French suddenly cancelled the programme, saying they did not need our design anymore. It was a great shock, making me re-live all the earlier disappointments I had faced—at Dehradun, when I failed to get into the IAF, and at Bangalore, when the *Nandi* project was aborted at ADE.

I had invested great hope and effort in the fourth stage, so that it could be flown with a *Diamont* rocket. The other three stages of the SLV, involving enormous work in the area of rocket propulsion were at least five years away. However, it did not take me long to shelve my disappointment over *Diamont*. After all, I had thoroughly enjoyed working on this project. In time, RATO filled the vaccuum created in me by the *Diamont*.

* * *

When the RATO project was underway, the SLV project slowly started taking shape. The capability to handle all major systems of a launch vehicle had been established in Thumba by now. Prof. Sarabhai once again demonstrated his mastery over the art of team-building. On one occasion, he had to identify a person who could be given the responsibility for developing a telecommand system for SLV-3. Two men were competent to carry out this task—one was the seasoned and sophisticated UR Rao, and the other a relatively unknown experimenter, G Madhavan Nair. I was deeply impressed by Madhavan Nair's dedication and abilities, but I did not rate his chances as very good.

On one of Prof. Sarabhai's routine visits, Madhavan Nair went out of his way to demonstrate his improvised but highly reliable telecommand system. Prof. Sarabhai did not take much time to back the young experimenter in preference to an established expert. Madhavan Nair not only lived up to the expectations of his leader; he even went beyond them. He was to later become the project director of the Polar Satellite Launch Vehicle (PSLV).

10. THE END OF AN ERA

Prof. Sarabhai's approach to mistakes rested on the assumption that they were inevitable but generally manageable. Once, when he came to Thumba on one of his routine visits, he was shown the operation of the nose cone jettisoning mechanism. We requested Prof. Sarabhai to formally activate the system. To our horror, nothing happened when he pressed the button. We were dumbstruck. In a flash, each of us mentally reviewed the failure.

We asked him to wait for a few minutes while we reforged some connections. When he pressed the button for the second time, the pyros were fired and the nose cone was jettisoned. Prof. Sarabhai congratulated us, but his expression suggested that his thoughts were elsewhere. The suspense did not last for long and I got a call from Prof. Sarabhai's secretary to meet him after dinner for an important discussion.

I was slightly perplexed by the summons. Prof. Sarabhai greeted me with his customary warmth at the Kovalam Palace Hotel, his usual home whenever he was in Trivandrum. He talked of the rocket launching station, facilities like launch pads, block houses, radar, telemetry and so on—things which are taken for granted in Indian space research today. Then he brought up the incident that had occurred that morning.

This was exactly what I had feared. But, there was no reproach from my leader. Instead, he put his finger on the key of the problem. We lacked a single roof to carry out system integration of all our rocket stages and rocket systems. There was little effort to bring together the disparate electrical and mechanical work. Prof. Sarabhai spent the next hour in re-defining our tasks, and, in the small hours of the morning, a decision to set up the Rocket Engineering Section was taken.

Mistakes can delay or prevent the proper achievement of the objectives of individuals and organisations, but a visionary like Prof. Sarabhai could use errors to encourage new ideas. I later realised, by experience, that the best way to prevent errors was to anticipate them. But this time by a strange twist of fate, the failure of the timer circuit led to the birth of a rocket engineering laboratory.

✳ ✳ ✳

I used to brief Prof. Sarabhai after every Missile Panel meeting. After attending one such meeting in New Delhi on 30 December 1971, I was returning to Trivandrum. Prof. Sarabhai was visiting

Thumba that very day to review the SLV design. I spoke to him on the telephone from the airport lounge in New Delhi, and we discussed the salient points that had emerged at the meeting. He instructed me to wait at Trivandrum airport and meet him there before his departure for Bombay the same night.

When I reached Trivandrum, a pall of gloom hung in the airport. The aircraft ladder operator, Kutty, told me in a choked voice that Prof. Sarabhai was no more. He had passed away a few hours ago, following a cardiac arrest. I was shocked to the core. All this had happened within an hour of our conversation. It was a great blow to me personally, and a huge loss to Indian science.

I remember an incident which occurred while Prof. Sarabhai was reviewing the bi-monthly progress of the design projects of SLV-3 in June 1970. Presentations on Stages I to IV were arranged. The first three presentations went through smoothly. Mine was the last presentation. I introduced five of my team members who had contributed in various ways to the design. To everybody's surprise, each of them presented his portion of the work with authority and confidence.

Suddenly, a senior scientist who worked closely with Prof. Sarabhai turned to me and enquired, "The presentations for your project were made by your team members based on their work. What have you done for the project?"

That was the first time I saw Prof. Sarabhai really annoyed. He told his colleague, "You ought to know what project management is all about. We just witnessed an excellent example. It was an outstanding demonstration of team-work. I have always seen a project leader as an integrator of people, and that is precisely what Kalam is."

I consider Prof. Sarabhai the mahatma of Indian science—a towering figure whose vision defined the country's space programme. He generated leadership qualities in his team and inspired them through both idea and example. For five years, between 1966 and 1971, about 22 scientists and engineers had worked closely with Prof. Sarabhai. All of them were later to take charge of important scientific projects.

As a tribute to the man to whom it owed its existence, the whole complex at Thumba was merged together to form an integrated space centre, and christened the Vikram Sarabhai Space Centre (VSSC). The renowned metallurgist, Dr. Brahm Prakash, took over as the first director of VSSC.

Less than a year after Prof. Sarabhai's death, the RATO system was successfully tested on 8 October 1972 at Bareilly Air Force Station in Uttar Pradesh. A high performance *Sukhoi-16* aircraft became airborne after a short run of 1200 m, as against its usual run of 2000 m. This effort was said to have saved approximately Rs. 4 crore in foreign exchange. Including trial expenses, we spent less than Rs. 25 lakh on the entire project. The Indian RATO could be produced at Rs. 17,000 apiece; replacing the imported RATO, which cost Rs. 33,000. The vision of Prof. Vikram Sarabhai, India's industrialist scientist, had finally borne fruit!

---

11. LEADING A TEAM

At the Vikram Sarabhai Space Centre, work on the SLV-3 went on at full swing. Prof. Satish Dhawan (who had steered ISRO for a while) in consultation with Dr. Brahm Prakash, appointed me Project Manager-SLV. My first task was to work out a project management plan.

I was aware of the contradiction that often occurred in missions which involved a large number of people. People heading teams

often have one of the following orientations—for some, work is
the most important motivation; for others, the workers form the
all-consuming interest. There are many others who fall either
between these two positions or outside them altogether. I fell
between; determined to prevent people from taking either extreme,
and to promote conditions where both work and workers went
together. I visualised my team as a group in which each member
worked to enrich the others in the team and enjoyed the experience
of working together.

The primary objectives of the SLV-3 project were design,
development and operation of a standard SLV system, capable of
reliably launching a 40-kg satellite into a 400-km circular orbit
around the earth.

I took up the responsibility of implementing the project within
the framework of policy decisions and also within the budget. Dr.
Brahm Prakash formed four Project Advisory Committees under
the guidance of several outstanding scientists, to advise me on
specialised areas. A target of an 'all line' flight test within 64
months was set in March 1973.

We made three groups to carry out the project activities—a
Programme Management Group, an Integration and Flight
Testing Group and a Subsystems Development Group. I projected
a requirement of 275 engineers and scientists for SLV-3, but could
get only about 50. If it had not been for the synergistic efforts of
these few, the whole project would have remained a non-starter.
Some young engineers developed their own ground rules to help
them work efficiently as a team, and produced outstanding
individual and team results.

Each member of the SLV-3 project team was a specialist in her or
his own field. It was natural, therefore, that each one of them
valued independence. To manage the performance of such

specialists, the team leader has to adopt a delicate balance between the hands-on and the hands-off approach. The hands-on approach means taking an active interest in the team's work, on a very regular basis. The hands-off approach trusts team members and recognises their need for autonomy, to carry out their roles as they see fit. It hinges on their self-motivation. When a leader goes too far with the hands-on approach, she or he is seen as an anxious and interfering type. But getting too hands-off can be seen as abandoning responsibility or not being interested.

Today, the members of the SLV-3 team have grown to lead some of the country's most prestigious programmes. Each one of these people rose to their present position through consistent hard work and will power. It was indeed an exceptionally talented team.

⁂ ⁂ ⁂

Having taken up the leadership of executing the SLV-3 project, I faced urgent and conflicting demands on my time—committee work, material procurement, correspondence, reviews, briefings, and the need to be informed on a wide range of subjects.

My day would start with a stroll of about two kilometres around the lodge I was living in. I used to prepare a general schedule during my morning walk, and emphasise the two or three things I would definitely like to accomplish during the day.

Once in the office, I would clear the table first. Within the next ten minutes, I would scan all the papers and quickly divide them into different categories—high priority, low priority, can be kept pending, and reading material. Then I would put the high priority papers in front of me and everything else out of sight.

Coming back to SLV-3, about 250 sub-assemblies and 44 major subsystems were conceived during the design. The list of materials went up to over one million components! A project implementation strategy had become essential to sustain this complex programme, which was expected to cover seven to ten years.

But, before I dwell on the finer aspects of the management of the SLV-3 project, let me talk about SLV-3 itself.

It is interesting to describe a launch vehicle using the human body in comparison. Imagine the main mechanical structure as the body of a human being. The control and guidance systems, with their electronic circuit systems, constitute the brain. The propellants form the muscle systems.

The self-sufficiency to produce SLV-3 came gradually, and not always without pain. We were a team of almost self-trained engineers. In retrospect, I feel the unique blend of our untutored talent, character, and dedication suited SLV-3 the most. I recall writing this after winding up a late-night shift:

> Beautiful hands are those that do
> Work that is earnest and brave and true
> Moment by moment the long day through.

✳ ✳ ✳

SLVs and missiles can be called first cousins. They are different in concept and purpose, but come from the same lineage— rocketry. A massive missile development project had been taken up by DRDO at the Defence Research and Development Laboratory (DRDL), Hyderabad. It had to do with the development of an indigenous surface-to-air missile.

The RATO project had been abandoned because the aircraft for which it was designed became obsolete, and the newly commissioned aircraft did not need RATO. With the project called off, Narayanan was the logical choice of the Defence Research and Development Organisation (DRDO) to lead the team that was to make the new missile. By now promoted to Air Commodore, Narayanan took over as Director, DRDL. He mobilised this young laboratory—located in the southeastern suburbs of Hyderabad—to take up this enormous task. The picturesque landscape, dotted with tombs and old buildings, buzzed with new life. Narayanan was a man of tremendous energy. He gathered around him a strong group of enthusiastic people.

Totally preoccupied with SLV-3 affairs, my participation in the Missile Panel meetings gradually dwindled, and then stopped altogether. However, stories about Narayanan and his project, code-named *Devil*, were beginning to reach Trivandrum. A transformation of an unprecedented scale was taking place there.

Back home at VSSC, SLV-3 was taking shape. In contrast to DRDL, which was sprinting ahead, we were moving slowly. Instead of following the leader, my team was trekking towards success on several individual paths. The essence of our method of work was an emphasis on communication—particularly in the lateral direction, among the teams and within the teams. In a way, communication was my mantra for managing this gigantic project.

Most of the time, communication gets confused with conversation. In fact, the two are distinctly different. I was (and still am) a terrible conversationalist, but consider myself a good communicator. A conversation full of pleasantries could be devoid of any useful information, whereas communication is meant only for the exchange of information. It is very important to realise that communication is a two-party affair which aims at passing on or receiving a specific piece of information.

While working on SLV-3, I defined the problems that existed and identified the action necessary to be taken to solve them through genuine communication. How did I do that? To begin with, I tried to be factual and never sugarcoated the bitter pill of facts. At one of the Space Science Council (SSC) review meetings, frustrated by the procurement delays, I complained agitatedly about the bureaucracy practised by the controller of accounts and financial advisor of VSSC. I insisted that the systems of work followed by the accounts staff had to change and demanded the delegation of their functions to the project team. Dr. Brahm Prakash was taken aback by my bluntness.

I spent the whole night regretting the pain my harsh words must have caused. However, I was determined to fight the inertia built into the system before I found myself being dragged down with it. Fortunately for me, Dr. Brahm Prakash delegated financial powers directly to the project the next morning.

※ ※ ※

Anyone who has taken up the responsibility to lead a team can be successful only by being sufficiently independent and powerful in her or his own right. What can one do to strengthen personal freedom? I would like to share two techniques I adopt.

The first is to build your education and skills. Knowledge is a tangible asset, quite often the most important tool in your work. The more up-to-date the knowledge you possess, the more free you are. Knowledge cannot be taken away from anyone. To lead, in a way, is to engage in continuing education. I understand that many professionals often go to college several nights every week, so that they do not lose track of current trends. To be a successful team leader, one has to stay back after the din and clutter of a working day to review the work done and emerge better-equipped to face a new day.

The second way is to develop a passion for personal responsibility. Be active! Take on responsibility! Work for the things you believe in.

The truth is that there is a great deal that most of us can individually do to increase our freedom. We can fight the forces that threaten to oppress us. We can strengthen ourselves with the qualities and conditions that promote individual freedom. In strengthening ourselves we help to create a stronger organisation, capable of achieving truly wonderful goals.

* * *

As work on SLV-3 gained momentum, Prof. Dhawan started reviewing progress with the entire team involved in the project. These review meetings were major events for all of us on the team. Prof. Dhawan was a man with a mission. He would effortlessly pull together all the loose ends for work to move smoothly. Yet, he never pretended to know more than he did. Instead, when something appeared ambiguous, he would ask questions and discuss his doubts frankly. I remember him as a firm but fair leader.

I had the privilege of spending a great deal of time with Prof. Dhawan. He could hold the listener enthralled with his logic and intellectual acumen. Debates with him were very stimulating and could always mentally energise my team members and I.

In 1975, ISRO became a government body. An ISRO Council was formed, consisting of directors from different work centres and senior officers in the Department of Space (DoS). The new set-up introduced me to TN Seshan, the joint secretary of the DoS. Till then, I had some reservations where bureaucrats were concerned, so I was not very comfortable when I first saw Seshan participating in a meeting. But soon, it changed to admiration as Seshan would always come for meetings prepared. He used to kindle the minds of scientists with his tremendous analytical capability.

The first three years of the SLV project were a revelation of the many fascinating mysteries of science. Being human, it is difficult to understand that ignorance has always been with us, and always will be. What was new was my awareness to this fact. I used to wrongly suppose that the function of science was to explain everything, and that unexplained phenomena were the province of mystics—people like my father and Lakshmana Sastry.

Gradually, I became aware of the difference between science and technology, between research and development. Science is inherently open-ended and exploratory. Development is encased in its objective.

I cautioned my team against becoming scientists. Science is a passion—a never-ending voyage into promises and possibilities. We had only limited time and limited funds. Making the SLV depended upon our awareness of our own limits. I preferred that we seek existing workable solutions. New demands enter time-bound projects creating their own problems—our job was to work around these problems and meet our target.

As participants in the SLV-3 project, we set three milestones for ourselves—development and flight qualification of all subsystems through sounding rockets by 1975; sub-orbital flights by 1976; and the final orbital flight in 1978. The work tempo had picked up now and the atmosphere was charged with excitement. Wherever I went, our teams had something interesting to show me. A large number of things were being done for the first time in the country and the ground-level technicians had no prior exposure to this kind of work. These were original performances put forth by my team members.

In June 1974, we used the *Centaur* sounding rocket launch to test some of our critical systems. None of them had ever been tried before in the country. The test was a huge success. Until then, the Indian space programme had not gone beyond sounding rockets and even knowledgeable people were not ready to see and acknowledge its efforts as anything more serious than fiddling around with meteorological instruments.

For the first time, we inspired the confidence of the nation. Prime Minister Indira Gandhi told Parliament on 24 July 1974, "The development and fabrication of relevant technologies, subsystems and hardware [to make India's first satellite launch vehicle] are progressing satisfactorily. A number of industries are engaged in the fabrication of components. The first orbital flight by India is scheduled to take place in 1978."

12.   Dear Ones Pass On

Working on SLV-3 was not without its painful moments, some of them at the personal level. One day, when my team and I were engrossed in work, the news of a death in the family reached me. My brother-in-law and mentor, Ahmed Jallaludin, was no more. For a couple of minutes, I stood motionless—I could not think, could not feel anything. When I could focus on my surroundings once more, I found myself talking incoherently.

Images from my childhood reappeared before me—evening walks around the Rameswaram temple; the shining sand and dancing tides; Jallaluddin showing me the horizon; arranging money for my books; seeing me off at Bombay airport when I left for NASA. My father, by now more than a hundred years old, and my sister Zohara—these images flashed before me, too terrible for me to comprehend. I composed myself and left instructions with my deputy to carry on with the work in my absence.

Travelling overnight in a combination of district buses, I reached Rameswaram only the next day. The moment I reached my house, grief hit me afresh. I had no words for Zohara, who was crying uncontrollably. My father held my hands for a long time.

Death has never frightened me. After all, everyone has to go one day. But perhaps Jallaluddin went a little too early, a little too soon. I could not bring myself to stay for long at home. For many days, back in Thumba, I felt a sense of futility I had never known before.

✳ ✳ ✳

I had long talks with Prof. Dhawan. He consoled me and said that progress on the SLV project would bring me solace from the grief. He drew my attention away from the tragedy and made me focus instead on the wonders of technology and our achievements.

Gradually, hardware had begun to emerge from the drawing boards. Each member of our team had a unique contribution to make. Sasi Kumar built a very effective network of fabrication work centres. Namboodiri and Pillai spent their days and nights developing four rocket motors simultaneously. MSR Dev and Sandlas drew up meticulous plans for mechanical and electrical integration of the vehicle. Madhavan Nair and Murthy examined the electronic systems and engineered them into flight sub-systems wherever it was possible. US Singh brought up the first launch ground system. He also chalked out a detailed work plan for the flight trials. Dr. Sundararajan closely monitored mission objectives and updated the systems.

In 1976, another tragedy struck. My father passed away at the age of one hundred and two. He had been in poor health for quite some time.

The death of Jallaluddin had taken its toll on my father's health and spirit. He seemed to have lost his desire to live, as though after seeing Jallaluddin return to his divine source, he too had become eager to return to his.

Whenever I had learned about my father's indifferent health, I would visit Rameswaram with a good city doctor. Every time I did so, he would chide me for my unnecessary concern and lecture me on the expenses incurred on the doctor.

"Your visit is enough for me to get well. Why bring a doctor and spend money?" he would ask.

But this time he had gone beyond the capabilities of any doctor. My father, Jainulabdeen, who had lived in Rameswaram for over one hundred years, passed away, leaving behind fifteen grandchildren and one great-grandson.

I sat for a long time with my mother, but could not speak. When I was preparing to leave, she blessed me in a voice choking with emotion. She knew that it was probably a final parting.

Was I excessively preoccupied with SLV-3? Should I have forgotten my own affairs for a while in order to be with her?

The SLV-3 apogee rocket, scheduled to be flight tested in France was mired in problems, and I was scheduled to rush to France to sort them out. Before I could leave, late in the afternoon, I was informed that my mother, too, had passed away.

I rushed to Rameswaram. Through the journey, an inspiring line in the Koran filled my mind, "Your wealth and children are only a temptation. Whereas Allah! With Him is eternal reward."

The next morning I was back at Thumba, physically exhausted, emotionally shattered, but determined to fulfil our ambition of flying an Indian rocket motor.

13. WORK BRINGS SOLACE

On my return from France, after successfully testing the SLV-3 apogee motor, Dr. Brahm Prakash informed me one day that Wernher von Braun would be visiting Thumba. I was to pick him up in Madras.

Everybody working in rocketry knows of von Braun, who made the lethal *V-2* missiles that devastated London in World War II. In the final stages of the war, von Braun was captured by the Allied forces. As a tribute to his genius, von Braun was given a top position in the rocketry programme at NASA. Working for the US Army, von Braun produced the landmark *Jupiter* missile, which was the first IRBM with a 3,000-km range.

The *V-2* missile was by far the greatest single achievement in the history of rockets and missiles. It was the culmination of the efforts of von Braun and his team in the VFR (Society for Space Flight, in Germany) in the 1920s. What had begun as a civilian effort soon became an official army one, and von Braun became the technical director of the German Missile Laboratory at Kummersdorf. The first *V-2* missile was tested unsuccessfully in June 1942. It toppled over on to its side and exploded. But on 16 August 1942, it became the first missile to exceed the speed of sound.

It filled me with awe that I would be travelling with this man—a scientist, designer, production engineer, administrator and technology manager, all rolled into one.

The *Avro* aircraft I brought him in took around ninety minutes from Madras to Trivandrum. Through the flight, von Braun asked me about our work and listened as if he was just another student

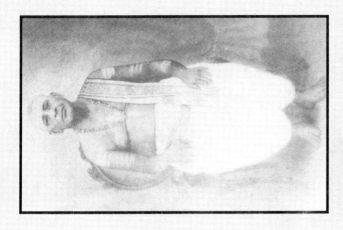

Pakshi Lakshmana Sastry, the head priest of the Shiva temple, and a close friend of my father's.

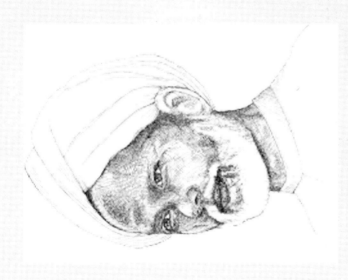

My father, Jainulabdeen, was a man of great wisdom and kindness.

Plate 1

Plate 2

My house on Mosque Street.

Plate 3

The Shiva temple at Rameswaram. My brother, Kasim Mohamed, ran a shop selling artefacts on this street and I often helped him at the shop.

The old mosque after which Mosque Street was named. My father brought my brothers and I here every evening.

Plate 4

Schwartz High School in Ramanathapuram. The words on the plaque say, "Let not thy winged days be spent in vain. When once gone, no gold can buy them back again."

Iyadurai Solomon (standing, left), my teacher at Schwartz High School, who taught me that with the benefits of a good education, I could aspire to become whatever I wished.

Plate 5

My brother, pointing at the T-square I used while studying at MIT.

Plate 6

Nandi, the hovercraft prototype, developed at ADE, Bangalore.

Plate 7

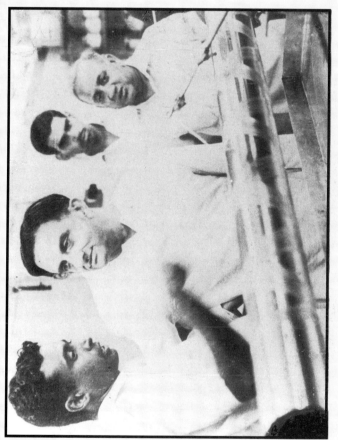

With Prof. Vikram Sarabhai (centre), the architect of India's space and missile development programmes. I stand to the left of the photograph.

Plate 8

St. Mary Magdalene church at Thumba, which housed the first unit of the space research centre.

Plate 9

Members of my SLV-3 team.

At one of the SLV-3 review meetings. Prof. Satish Dhawan sits to the right,
while Dr. Brahm Prakash sits to the left.

Plate 10

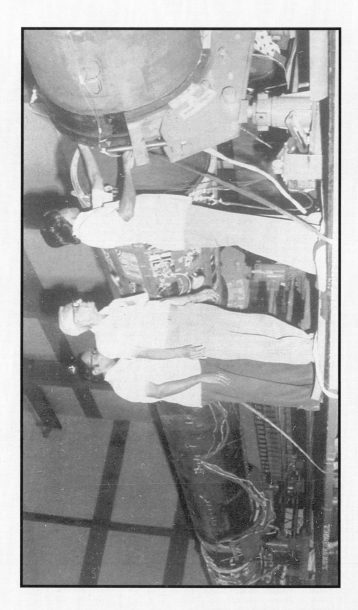

Dr. Brahm Prakash inspecting SLV-3 in its final phase of integration.

Plate 11

SLV-3 on the launch pad. This gave us many anxious moments!

Plate 12

Prof. Satish Dhawan and I explain SLV-3 results to Prime Minister Indira Gandhi.

Receiving the Padma Bhushan from Dr. Sanjeeva Reddy, then President of India.

of rocketry. I never expected the father of modern rocketry to be so humble, receptive and encouraging. He made me feel comfortable right through the flight.

How did he feel in the US? I asked this of von Braun, who had become a cult figure in America after creating the *Saturn* rocket in the *Apollo* mission (which put the first man on the moon).

"America is a country of great possibilities, but they look upon everything un-American with suspicion and contempt. They suffer from a deep-rooted NIH—Not Invented Here—complex, and look down on alien technologies. If you want to do anything in rocketry, do it yourself," von Braun advised me.

He continued, "SLV-3 is a genuine Indian design and you may be having your own troubles. But you should always remember that one doesn't just build on successes, but also on failures. Mere hard work cannot fetch you honour. Building a rock wall is backbreaking work. There are some people who build rock walls all their lives. And when they die, they leave behind miles of walls, mute testimony to how hard they had worked.

"But there are others who, while placing one rock on top of another, have a vision. It may be to create a terrace with roses climbing over the rock walls and chairs set out for lazy summer days. Or the rock wall may enclose an apple orchard or mark a boundary. What matters is that when they finish, they have more than a wall. It is this goal that makes the difference.

"Do not make rocketry your profession or your livelihood—make it your religion, your mission."

Did I see something of Prof. Vikram Sarabhai in Wernher von Braun? It made me happy to think so.

With three deaths in the family in as many years, I needed total commitment to my work in order to keep performing. I wanted to throw all my being into creating the SLV. During this period, it was as though I had pushed a 'hold' button on my life—no badminton in the evenings, no more weekends or holidays, no family, no relations, not even any friends outside the SLV circle.

To succeed in your mission, you must have single-minded devotion to your goal. Individuals like myself are often called 'workaholics'. I question this term because that implies an illness. If I work towards that which I desire more than anything else in the world, and which also makes me happy, how can it be considered an aberration?

The desire to work at optimum capacity leaves hardly any room for anything else. I have had people with me who would scoff at the 40-hours-a-week job they were paid for. I have also known others who worked 60, 80 and even 100 hours a week because they found their work exciting and rewarding. Total commitment is the common denominator among all successful men and women.

Once you have done this—charged yourself, as it were, with your commitment to your work—you also need good health and boundless energy. Climbing to the top demands strength—whether to the top of Mount Everest or to the top of your career.

'Flow' is an overwhelming and joyous experience while working—it is a sensation we experience when we act with total involvement. During flow, action follows action according to an internal logic; there seems to be no need of conscious intervention on the part of the worker. There is no hurry and there are no distracting demands on one's attention. The distinction between self and the activity disappears.

All of us working on SLV were experiencing flow. Although we were working very hard, we were very relaxed, energetic and fresh. How did it happen? Who had created this flow? Perhaps it was the fact that the difficult targets we had set actually seemed achievable.

When the SLV-3 hardware started emerging, our ability to concentrate increased markedly. I felt a tremendous surge of confidence—I was in complete control over myself and over the SLV-3 project.

The first requirement to get into flow is to work as hard as you can at something that presents a challenge. It may not be an overwhelming challenge, but one that stretches you a little; something that makes you realise that you are performing a task better today than you did yesterday, or the last time you tried to do it.

Another pre-requisite for being in flow is the availability of a significant span of uninterrupted time. In my experience, it is difficult to switch into the flow state in less than half an hour. And it is almost impossible if you are disturbed constantly.

I have experienced this state many times, almost every day of the SLV-3 mission. There have been days in the laboratory when I have looked up to find the laboratory empty and realised that it was way past my work hours. On other days, my team members and I have been so caught up in our work that the lunch hour slipped by without our even being conscious that we were hungry.

---

14.   SETBACKS, FAILURES AND FRIENDS

We had scheduled the first experimental flight trial of SLV-3 for 10 August 1979. The primary goals of the mission were to realise a fully integrated launch vehicle and to evaluate on-board systems as well as the ground system. The 23-metre-long, four-stage SLV rocket, weighing 17 tonnes, finally took off elegantly at 0758 hours and immediately started following its programmed trajectory.

Stage I performed to perfection. There was a smooth transition from this stage to Stage II. We were spellbound to see our hopes flying. But suddenly, the spell was broken. Stage II went out of control. The flight was terminated after 317 seconds and the vehicle's remains—including Stage IV with the payload—crashed into the sea, 560 km off Sriharikota.

The incident caused us profound disappointment. I felt a strange mix of anger and frustration.

The premature death of my hovercraft *Nandi*, the abandoning of the RATO, the abortion of the *Diamont's* fourth stage all came alive in a flash. Over the years, I had somehow learned to absorb the abortion of these endeavours, had come to terms with them and gone on to pursue fresh dreams. That day, I re-lived each one of those setbacks in my misery.

I had hardly had any sleep in the week prior to the launch. Completely drained—mentally, as well as physically—I went straight to my room and slumped onto the bed.

A gentle touch on my shoulder woke me up. It was late in the afternoon, almost approaching evening. I saw Dr. Brahm Prakash sitting by my bedside. "What about going for lunch?" he asked.

I was deeply touched by his affection and concern. I found out later that he had come to my room twice before that, but had gone away on finding me asleep. He had waited all that time for me to have lunch with him! Dr. Brahm Prakash made light conversation during the meal, carefully avoiding the topic of SLV-3.

Later, he called upon the SLV team and demonstrated to me that I was not alone in my sorrow at SLV-3's failure. "All your colleagues stand by you," he said. This gave me vital emotional support and guidance, knowing that the entire team shared my sorrow.

A post-flight review was attended by more than seventy scientists, all of whom were keen to pin-point the reasons for the malfunctioning of the vehicle. It was established that the mishap occurred because of the failure of Stage II's control system. No control force was available at this stage of the flight, and this caused the vehicle to fall into the sea even before the other stages could ignite.

The findings were presented to Prof. Dhawan at a meeting of top ISRO scientists. Everybody was convinced by the technical cause-and-effect sequence presented and there was a general feeling of satisfaction about the whole exercise. I was unconvinced though and felt restless.

On the spur of the moment, I stood up and said that, as the mission director, I should have put the launch on hold and saved the flight if possible. "In a similar situation abroad, the mission director would have lost his job. I therefore take responsibility for SLV-3's failure," I announced. For some time there was total silence in the hall.

Then Prof. Dhawan got up and said "I am going to put Kalam in orbit!" He left the place signalling that the meeting was over.

The pursuit of science is a combination of great elation and great despair. I went over many instances in my mind, such as Johannes Kepler and von Braun, whose *Saturn* launch vehicle put man on the moon. I thought of their failures and frustration. These thoughts helped to give me the ability to withstand apparently irreversible setbacks.

✳ ✳ ✳

Early in November 1979, Dr. Brahm Prakash retired. He had always been my sheet-anchor. His belief in team spirit had inspired the management pattern for the SLV project, which later became a blueprint for all scientific projects in the country.

Dr. Brahm Prakash not only reinforced the traits which I had acquired from Prof. Sarabhai, but also helped me give them new dimensions. He always cautioned me against haste, saying, "Big scientific projects are like mountains, which should be climbed without urgency. It is like climbing a mountain to reach the peak without experiencing its sides. The sides of the mountain sustain life, not the peak. This is where things grow, experience is gained, and technologies are mastered. The importance of the peak lies only in the fact that it defines the sides."

15. SUCCESS AT LAST!

On 17 July 1980, 30 hours before the launch of the second SLV-3, the newspapers were filled with all kinds of predictions. One newspaper reported, "The mission director is missing and could not be contacted."

Many reports preferred to trace the history of the first SLV-3 flight, and recalled how the rocket had nosedived into the sea; others detailed all that ailed our country and related it to the SLV-3. I knew that the next day's launch was going to decide the future of the Indian space programme. Quite simply, the eyes of the whole nation were on us.

In the early hours of 18 July 1980, at 0803 hrs to be precise, India's first satellite launch vehicle, SLV-3 lifted off from SHAR.

I spoke amidst the screeching decibels, the most important words I had ever uttered in my life, "Mission Director calling all stations. Stand by for an important announcement. All stages performed to mission requirements. The fourth stage apogee motor has given the required velocity to put *Rohini* satellite into orbit."

There were happy cries everywhere. When I came out of the block house, I was lifted onto the shoulders of my jubilant colleagues and carried in a procession.

The whole nation was excited. India had entered the small group of nations which possessed satellite launch capability. Newspapers carried reports of the event in their headlines. Radio and television stations aired special programmes. Parliament greeted the achievement with the thumping of desks. It was both the culmination of a national dream, and the beginning of a very important phase in our nation's history.

Prof. Satish Dhawan, chairman of ISRO, announced that it was now well within our ability to explore space. Prime Minister Indira Gandhi cabled her congratulations. But the most important reaction was that of the Indian scientific community—everybody was proud of this one hundred per cent indigenous effort.

The credit for the successful SLV-3 flight goes, first, to the giants of the Indian space programme—Prof. Sarabhai in particular, who had envisioned this effort; next, to the hundreds of VSSC personnel who had, through sheer will-power, proved their mettle; and Prof. Dhawan and Dr. Brahm Prakash, who had led the project.

I experienced mixed feelings. I was happy to achieve the success which had been evading me for the past two decades, but I was sad because the people who had inspired me were no longer there to share my joy—my parents, my brother-in-law Jallaluddin, and Prof. Sarabhai.

We had a late dinner that evening. Gradually, the din and clatter of the celebrations calmed down and I retired to my bed with almost no energy left.

Within a month of the success, I visited the Nehru Science Centre in Bombay for a day, in response to an invitation to share my experiences. There, I received a telephone call from Prof. Dhawan in New Delhi, asking me to join him the next morning. We were to meet Prime Minister Indira Gandhi.

My hosts at the Nehru Centre were kind enough to arrange my ticket to Delhi. But, I had a problem. It had to do with my clothes. I was dressed casually as usual, wearing slippers—not, by any standards of etiquette, suitable attire in which to meet the prime minister!

When I told Prof. Dhawan about this problem, he told me not to worry about my dress. "You are beautifully clothed in your success," he quipped.

Prof. Dhawan and I arrived at Parliament House Annexe the next morning. A meeting of the parliamentary panel on science and technology, chaired by the prime minister, was scheduled. There were about 30 members of the Lok Sabha and Rajya Sabha in the room, which was lit by a majestic chandelier. Prof. MGK Menon and Dr. Nag Chaudhuri were also present.

The prime minister spoke to the members about the success of the SLV-3 and lauded our achievement. Prof. Dhawan thanked the gathering for the encouragement given by them to space research in the country and expressed the gratitude of the ISRO scientists and engineers.

Then, Mrs. Gandhi said, "Kalam! We would like to hear you speak." I was surprised by the request.

Hesitantly, I rose and said, "I am indeed honoured to be in this great gathering of nation-builders. I only know how to build a rocket system in our country, which can inject a satellite, built in our country, by imparting to it a velocity of 25,000 km per hour."

There was thunderous applause. I thanked the members for giving us an opportunity to work on a project like SLV-3 and prove the scientific strength of our country. The entire room radiated happiness.

✳ ✳ ✳

Now that SLV-3 had been successfully completed, VSSC had to re-organise its resources and redefine its goals. I wanted to be relieved of project activities. Consequently, Ved Prakash Sandlas from my team was made the project director for the SLV-3 Continuation Project, which aimed at making operational satellite launch vehicles of a similar class.

With a view to upgrading the SLV-3 by means of certain technological innovations, the development of Augmented satellite launch vehicles (ASLVs) had been on the anvil for some time. The aim was to enhance the SLV-3 payload capability from 40 kg to 50 kg. MSR Dev from my team was appointed Project Director, ASLV.

Then, to reach the sun-synchronous orbit (900 km), a Polar satellite launch vehicle (PSLV) was to be made. The Geosynchronous satellite launch vehicle (GSLV) was also envisaged, though as a distant dream. I took up the position of Director, Aerospace Dynamics and Design Group, so that I could configure the forthcoming launch vehicles and technology development.

The existing VSSC infrastructure was inadequate to handle the size and weight of the future launch vehicle systems. The implementation of all these projects was going to require highly specialised facilities. New sites were identified for the expanded activities of VSSC at Vaattiyoorkavu and Valiamala.

Fresh planning and analysis, especially of facilities, started. Some of the activity we undertook now paved the way for the formulation of the Re-entry experiment (REX) which, much later on, became *Agni*.

16.   MOVING ON

The next SLV-3 flight, SLV3-D1, took off on 31 May 1981. I witnessed this flight from the visitors' gallery. This was the first time I witnessed a launch from outside the control centre.

An unpalatable truth I had to face was that by becoming the focus of media attention, I had aroused the envy of some of my senior colleagues, all of whom had contributed equally to the success of SLV-3. Was I hurt at the coldness of the new environment? Perhaps yes, but I was willing to accept what I couldn't change.

I have never lived off the profits of another's mind. My life has never been that of a ruthless achiever. The SLV-3 was made, not through force, but through consistent, collective effort. Then why this sense of bitterness? Was it peculiar to the VSSC top level or a universal reality? This bitterness was real, and I had to reason it out.

In January 1981, I was invited by Dr. Bhagiratha Rao of the High Altitude laboratory (now the Defence Electronics Applications Laboratory or DEAL) in Dehradun to give a lecture on SLV-3.

The renowned nuclear scientist, Prof. Raja Ramanna, whom I had always admired, and who was then the scientific adviser to the defence minister, presided over the gathering. He spoke of India's efforts at generating nuclear energy and the challenge in conducting the first nuclear test for peaceful purposes. As I had been so closely involved with SLV-3, it was natural that I was soon intrigued by it. Later, Prof. Ramanna invited me for a private meeting over tea.

The first thing that struck me when I met Prof. Ramanna was his genuine pleasure at meeting me. There was an eagerness in his talk, an immediate, sympathetic friendliness, accompanied by quick, graceful movements. The evening brought back memories of my first meeting with Prof. Sarabhai. He did not take long to come to the point.

The *Devil* missile programme had been shelved in spite of tremendous achievements made by Narayanan and his team at DRDL. The entire programme of military rockets was reeling under persistent apathy. The DRDO needed somebody to take command of their missile programmes, which were stuck at the drawing board and static test bed stages. Prof. Ramanna asked me if I would like to join DRDL and shoulder the responsibility of shaping their guided missile development programme (GMDP).

Prof. Ramanna's proposal evoked a mixture of emotions in me. When again would I have such an opportunity to consolidate all our knowledge of rocketry and apply it?

I felt honoured by the esteem in which Prof. Ramanna held me. He had been the guiding spirit behind the Pokhran nuclear test (in 1974), and I was thrilled by his ability to draw the world's attention to India's technical competence. I knew I would not be able to refuse him. Prof. Ramanna advised me to talk to Prof. Dhawan and request him to work out the details of my transfer from ISRO to DRDL.

I met Prof. Dhawan on 14 January 1981. He gave me a patient hearing, weighing everything carefully to make sure he didn't miss a point. Finally, he said, "I am pleased with their appraisal of your work."

I wondered how I should proceed. "Should I formally apply for the post so that DRDL could send the appointment order?" I enquired of Prof. Dhawan.

"No. Don't pressurise them. Let me talk to the management during my next visit to Delhi," Prof. Dhawan said. He added, "I know you have always had one foot in DRDO. Now your whole centre of gravity seems to have shifted towards them."

Perhaps what Prof. Dhawan was telling me had an element of truth in it. But my heart had always been at ISRO. Was he really unaware of that? Eighteen years at ISRO was too long a stay to leave without pain.

Meanwhile, Republic Day of 1981 had brought with it a pleasant surprise. Mahadevan, secretary to Prof. UR Rao, rang up from New Delhi to tell me of the Home Ministry's announcement that the Padma Bhushan award was being conferred on me. Prof. Dhawan also called to congratulate me wholeheartedly. I then rang up Dr. Brahm Prakash and thanked him. Dr. Brahm Prakash chided me for the formality and said, "I feel as if my son has got the award." I was so deeply touched by Dr. Brahm Prakash's affection that I could no longer keep my emotions in check.

My Padma Bhushan got mixed reactions at VSSC. While there were some who shared my happiness, there were others who felt I was being unduly singled out for recognition. Some of my close associates turned envious.

---

17.   A NEW JOB AND A WEDDING

A minor tussle over my services occurred at this time, between ISRO, which was a little hesitant to relieve me, and DRDO, which wanted to take me in.

Many months went by, many letters were exchanged. Prof. Ramanna retired as the scientific adviser and was succeeded by Dr. VS Arunachalam. Overcoming the niggling doubts that had caused delays over the past year, the decision to appoint me director of DRDL was finally taken in February 1982.

Prof. Dhawan used to visit my room in the ISRO headquarters, and we spent many hours together. Before I left ISRO, Prof. Dhawan asked me to give a talk on the profile of the space programme in India by the year 2000. Almost all the ISRO management and staff attended my talk, which was by way of a farewell meeting.

I visited DRDL in April 1982 to acquaint myself with my potential work site. The then director of DRDL, SL Bansal, took me around and introduced me to the senior scientists in the laboratory.

Meanwhile, Anna University in Madras, conferred an honorary degree of Doctor of Science on me. I had acquired my degree in Aeronautical Engineering almost twenty years earlier and was happy that Anna University had recognised my efforts in the field of rocketry. But what pleased me most was the recognition of the value of our work in academic circles. To my delight, the honorary degree was awarded at a convocation presided over by Prof. Ramanna.

I joined DRDL on 1 June 1982. Very soon, I realised that this laboratory was still haunted by the winding up of the *Devil* missile project. Many excellent professionals had not yet recovered from the disappointment.

I realised that the burial of the *Devil* was essential for the rise of hope and vision. About a month later, Admiral OS Dawson visited DRDL, and I used his visit as an opportunity to make a point with my team.

I emphasised the sea-skimming role of the tactical core vehicle that was being developed. I focussed not on its technical intricacies, but on its battlefield capabilities. And I highlighted the production plans. The message was loud and clear to my new associates—do not make anything which you cannot sell later and do not spend your life making one thing only.

My first few months at DRDL were largely interactive. I not only described and explained our goals, but also the interplay between our work and ourselves.

I was astonished to see the determination of the DRDL workforce, who, in spite of the premature winding up of their earlier projects, were eager to go ahead. I arranged reviews for various subsystems.

To the horror of many old-timers in DRDO, I also extended invitations to people from the Indian Institute of Science, Indian Institutes of Technology, Council for Scientific and Industrial Research, Tata Institute of Fundamental Research, and many other educational institutions where related experts could be found. I felt that the stuffy work centres of DRDL needed a breath of fresh air.

ISRO was lucky to have had Prof. Sarabhai and Prof. Dhawan at the helm—leaders who highlighted their goals clearly, made their missions larger than their lives, and could then inspire their entire workforce. DRDL had not been so lucky.

In order to speed up the pace of R&D activities at DRDL, decisions on vital scientific, technical and technological problems had to be taken quickly. Throughout my career I had sincerely pursued openness in scientific matters. So the first major decision which we took was to create a forum of senior scientists where important matters could be discussed collectively. Thus, a high-level body called the Missile Technology Committee was formed within DRDL. We also evolved a programme by which middle-level scientists and engineers could be involved in the management activities of the laboratory.

After days of debate and thinking, the long-term guided missile development programme was drawn up. I had read somewhere,

"The great thing in the world is not knowing so much where we stand, as in what direction we are moving." So what if we did not have the technological might of the West? We knew we had to attain that might, and this determination was our driving force.

To draw up a clear and well-defined missile development programme for the production of indigenous missiles, a committee was constituted under my chairmanship. We drafted a paper for the Cabinet Committee for Political Affairs (CCPA) to study. The paper was given its final shape after consulting the representatives of the three defence services—the army, navy and air force. We estimated an expenditure of about Rs. 390 crore, spread over a period of twelve years.

Development programmes often get stuck by the time they reach the production stage, mainly because of lack of funding. We wanted to get funds to develop and produce two missiles— a low-level, quick-reaction tactical core vehicle, and a medium-range surface-to-surface weapons system. DRDL had been known for its pioneering work in the field of anti-tank missiles. We proposed to develop a third generation anti-tank guided missile having 'fire-and-forget' capabilities. All my colleagues were pleased with the proposal. They saw an opportunity to pursue fresh activities.

I made a presentation to the government which the defence minister presided over, and which was attended by the three service chiefs and senior officials. Everyone seemed to have all sorts of doubts—on our capabilities, the technological infrastructure, viability, schedule and cost. Dr. Arunachalam stood by me throughout the entire question-and-answer session. Although some questioned our ambitious proposal, everyone was very excited at the idea of India having her own missile systems. In the end, we were asked by Defence Minister R Venkataraman to meet him in the evening, about three hours later.

We spent the intervening time working out possibilities. If they sanctioned only Rs. 100 crore, how would we allocate it? Suppose they gave us Rs. 200 crore, then what would we do? When we met the defence minister in the evening, I had a hunch that we were going to get some funds at least.

But, when he suggested that we launch an integrated GMDP, instead of making missiles in phases, we could not believe our ears, and begged for time to rethink.

"Come back tomorrow morning, please, with your plan," the defence minister replied.

That night, Dr. Arunachalam and I laboured together to rework our plan. We worked out some important changes in our proposal. We took all the variables—such as design, fabrication, system integration, experimental flights, evaluation, updating, user trials, quality, reliability, and financial viability—into account. We wanted to deliver contemporary missiles to our defence services and not some outdated list of weapons. A very exciting challenge had been thrown to us.

By the time we finished our work, it was already morning. Suddenly, at the breakfast table, I remembered that I was to attend my niece Zameela's wedding at Rameswaram that evening. But, by then it was already too late to do anything. Even if I could catch the Madras flight later in the day, how would I reach Rameswaram from there? A pang of guilt dampened my spirits. Was it fair, I asked myself, to forget my family commitments and obligations? Zameela was more like a daughter to me. The thought of missing her wedding was very distressing. I finished breakfast and left for the meeting, since there was nothing I could do.

The defence minister was visibly pleased with our new proposal, which had turned overnight into the blueprint of an integrated programme with far-reaching consequences. It would have wide-ranging technological spin-offs, and was exactly what the defence minister had had in mind the previous evening. He cleared the entire proposal.

Soon after, the defence minister stood up, signalling that the meeting was over. I turned towards the door when I heard Dr. Arunachalam tell the minister about Zameela's wedding that evening at Rameswaram. I was overwhelmed when the minister located an air force helicopter to take me from Madras to Madurai. I left New Delhi for Madras an hour after our meeting was over, taking a regular Indian Airlines flight. Dr. Arunachalam told me, "You have earned this for your hard work of the last six months."

The air force helicopter was close to the Indian Airlines aircraft as it landed in Madras. Within the next few minutes I was on my way to Madurai. The commandant of the air force base there was kind enough to take me to the railway station, where the train to Rameswaram was just about to roll out of the platform. I was in Rameswaram well in time for Zameela's wedding. I blessed my brother's daughter with a father's love.

---

18. MAKING OUR OWN MISSILES

The defence minister put up our proposal before the Cabinet and saw it through. An unprecedented amount of Rs. 388 crore was sanctioned! Thus was born India's prestigious integrated guided missile development programme (IGMDP). When I presented the government's sanction letter before the Missile Technology Committee at DRDL, they were not only excited, but full of fire and action.

The proposed projects were christened in accordance with the spirit of India's self-reliance. Thus the surface-to-surface weapon system became *Prithvi* (earth) and the tactical core vehicle was called *Trishul* (the trident of Shiva). The surface-to-air area defence system was named *Akash* (sky) and the anti-tank missile project became *Nag* (cobra). I gave the name *Agni* (fire) to my long-cherished dream of the REX.

Dr. Arunachalam came to DRDL and formally launched IGMDP on 27 July 1983. It was a great event in which every single employee of DRDL participated. Everybody who was somebody in Indian aerospace research was invited. A large number of scientists from other laboratories and organisations, professors from academic institutions, representatives of the armed forces, and people from the production centres and inspection authorities (who were our business partners now) were present on this occasion. A closed-circuit TV network had to be used to ensure proper communication between the participants, for we had no single place to accommodate all the invitees! This was the second-most significant day in my career, next only to 18 July 1980, when SLV-3 had launched *Rohini* into the earth's orbit.

The launch of IGMDP was like a bright flash on the Indian scientific firmament. Missile technology had been considered the monopoly of a few select nations in the world. People were curious to see how India was going to achieve all that was promised. The magnitude of IGMDP was really unprecedented in the country. Getting the go-ahead and funds for the programme could at best be seen as only ten per cent of the work done. To get it going would be quite a different matter altogether.

During this period, the most important task before me was the selection of the project directors to lead individual missile projects. DRDL had a large pool of highly talented people, many of whom were, unfortunately, egotistical. The question was whom to pick—a go-getter, a planner, a maverick, a dictator or a team man? I had to get the right type of leader who could clearly visualise the goal and channelise the energies of the team members working at different work centres.

It was a difficult game, some rules of which I had learnt while working on ISRO's high-priority projects for two decades. The wrong choice would jeopardise the entire future of the programme. Many of my senior colleagues—naming them would be unfair, because it could be only my imagination—tried to befriend me during this period. I respected their concern for a lonely man, but avoided any close contacts. Through loyalty to a friend, one can be easily led into doing something that is not in the best interests of the organisation.

✳ ✳ ✳

My search for someone to lead the *Prithvi* project ended with Col. VJ Sundaram, who belonged to the EME corps of the Indian Army. He experimented with team work and had an extraordinary capability to evaluate alternative ways of operating. He would suggest moving forward into new terrains. I knew the project director of *Prithvi* would be the first to make decisions with production agencies and the armed forces—and Col. Sundaram would be the ideal choice to see that sound decisions were taken.

For *Trishul*, I was looking for someone who not only had a sound knowledge of electronics and missile warfare, but who could also communicate these complexities to the team in order to promote understanding and support. I found in Commodore SR Mohan, from the Indian Navy, a talent for detail and an almost magical power of persuasion.

For *Agni*, my dream project, I needed somebody who would tolerate my occasional meddling in the running of this project. In RN Agarwal I found the right person. He was an alumnus of MIT, with a brilliant academic record. He had been managing the aeronautical test facilities at DRDL.

Due to technological complexities, *Akash* and *Nag* were then considered missiles of the future; their activities were expected to peak about half a decade later. Therefore, I selected the relatively young Prahlada and NR Iyer.

In those days, issues of general importance could not be openly discussed or decisions debated. Therefore, I formulated the Science Council, a sort of panchayat, where the community would sit together and take common decisions. Every three months, all the scientists—juniors and seniors, veterans and freshers—would sit together and let off steam.

The very first meeting of the Council was eventful. After a spell of half-hearted enquiries and expressions of doubt, one senior scientist shot a straight question at me, "On what basis did you select these five Pandavas (he meant the project directors)?"

I was, in fact, expecting this question. I told him to wait and see. I had chosen them to take charge of long-term programmes where new storms would arise everyday.

One of the most difficult questions came from a young scientist, "How are you going to stop these projects from going the *Devil* way?"

I explained to him the philosophy behind IGMDP—it began with design and ended in deployment. The participation of production centres and user agencies had been ensured, and there was no question of going back till the missile systems had been successfully deployed in the battlefield.

✳ ✳ ✳

While the process of forming teams and organising work was going on, I found that the space available at DRDL was grossly inadequate to meet the new requirements of IGMDP. Some of the facilities would have to be located at another site.

I visited the nearby Imarat Kancha area. Decades ago, it had been a test range for anti-tank missiles developed by DRDL. The terrain was barren, there were hardly any trees, and the area was dotted with large boulders typical of the Deccan plateau. I felt the tremendous energy trapped in these stones and decided to locate the integration and check-out facilities needed for the missile projects here. For the next three years, this became my mission.

We drew up a proposal to establish a model high-technology research centre with very advanced technical facilities. By any standards, this was a gigantic task. An altogether different brand of expertise, grit and determination were required to realise this project. Who would be the most suitable person to do so? I saw almost all the required leadership qualities for this purpose in MV Suryakantha Rao.

According to the established procedure, we approached the Military Engineering Services (MES) for the construction work. They said it would take five years to complete the task. The matter was discussed in-depth at the highest level in the Ministry of Defence, and a landmark decision to entrust the responsibility to an outside construction company was taken. The Survey of India and the National Remote Sensing Agency collaborated with us at Imarat Kancha to prepare a layout for the approach roads and the location of the facilities. The Central Ground Water Board identified twenty locations amid the rocks to tap water. Infrastructure to provide 40 MVA power and 5 million litres of water per day was planned.

Now that we had started working on the design of the missile systems and development had already commenced, the next logical step was to look for a suitable site for the missile flight trials. With SHAR also in Andhra Pradesh, the search for a suitable site spread towards the eastern coastline, and finally ended at Balasore in Orissa. A site along the north-eastern coast was identified for a national test range.

The project at Balasore ran into rough weather because of political issues raised around the evacuation of people living in that area. We decided therefore to create an interim infrastructure at Chandipur, also in Orissa. Funding of Rs. 30 crore had been given to construct the range, called the interim test range (ITR). Sadly, our plans were to affect a beautiful bird sanctuary in Chandipur.

Creating the new centre at Imarat Kancha was perhaps the most satisfying experience of my life. Developing this centre of excellence of missile technology was akin to the joy of a potter shaping artefacts of lasting beauty. The infrastructure at Imarat Kancha would come to be known as Research Centre Imarat (RCI), retaining the original identity of the place.

Defence Minister R Venkataraman visited DRDL in September 1983 to evaluate the activities of IGMDP. He advised us to list all the resources we needed to achieve our goals, overlooking nothing, and then include our own positive imagination and faith in the list. Both Dr. Arunachalam and I saw endless possibilities stretching out before IGMDP, and our enthusiasm proved infectious. We were further encouraged to see the best professionals in the country gravitating towards IGMDP. The word had evidently got around that the IGMDP was a winner.

We were at a meeting laying down the targets for the year, when news came of Dr. Brahm Prakash's death on the evening of 3 January 1984 at Bombay. It was a great emotional loss for me, for I had had the privilege of working under him during the most challenging period of my career. His compassion and humility were exemplary. I remembered his healing touch on the day of the failed SLV flight, and my sorrow deepened further.

If Prof. Sarabhai was the creator of VSSC, Dr. Brahm Prakash was the executor. Dr. Brahm Prakash played a very important role in shaping my leadership skills. His humility had mellowed me and helped me control my aggressive approach.

❋ ❋ ❋

An altitude control system and an on-board computer developed by P Banerjee, KV Ramana Sai and their team was almost ready. The success of this effort is very vital for any indigenous missile development programme. All the same, we had to have a missile to test this important system.

After many brainstorming sessions, we decided to improvise a *Devil* missile to test the system. A *Devil* missile was taken apart, and the modified and extended range missile was fired with a make-shift launcher, on 26 June 1984, to flight test the guidance system. The system met all the requirements.

This was the first significant step in the history of Indian missile development. So far it had been restricted to reverse engineering. But now we were moving towards designing our own systems. The message was loud and clear. We could do it!

It did not take long for the message to reach New Delhi, and Prime Minister Indira Gandhi expressed her desire to personally apprise herself of the progress of IGMDP. The entire organisation was filled with an aura of excitement. On 19 July 1984, she visited DRDL. It was an honour to receive her at DRDL. Mrs. Gandhi was immensely conscious that she was the leader of eight hundred million people. Every step, every gesture, every movement of her hands reflected this. The esteem in which she held our work in the field of guided missiles boosted our morale immensely.

During the one hour that she spent at DRDL, she covered wide-ranging aspects of IGMDP—from flight system plants to multiple development laboratories. In the end, she addressed the 2000-strong DRDL community. She asked for the schedules of the flight system that we were working on and asked us when we were going to flight test *Prithvi*.

I answered, "June 1987."

She responded immediately, "Let me know what is needed to accelerate the flight schedule. A fast pace of work is the hope of the entire nation." She also told me that the emphasis of IGMDP should rest not only on the schedule, but also on excellence.

A large number of original ideas sprung up from the participating work centres. If you were to ask me to indicate the single most important managerial tactic in this successful programme, I would point to the rapid and pro-active follow-up. In fact, the work code in the guided missile programme office was—if you need to write a letter to a work centre, send a fax; if you need to send a telex or fax, telephone; and if the need arises for telephonic discussions, visit the place personally.

The power of this approach came to light when Dr. Arunachalam conducted a comprehensive status review of IGMDP on 27 September 1984.

It was a pleasure to find an old acquaintance, TN Seshan, on the review board. Between SLV-3 and now, we had developed a mutual affection. However, this time as the defence secretary, Seshan's queries about the schedules and viability of financial propositions presented were much more pointed. My team was particularly pleased to answer his questions about the advanced technology employed in IGMDP. I still remember his uncanny curiosity about everything. And to let you into a small secret, Seshan is perhaps the only person in the world who enjoys calling me by my full name which contains 31 letters and five words—Avul Pakir Jainulabdeen Abdul Kalam.

19. AN INFUSION OF YOUNG BLOOD

The missile programme had partners in design, development and production from 12 academic institutions and 30 laboratories—like DRDO, the Council of Scientific and Industrial Research (CSIR), ISRO, etc. In fact, more than fifty professors and one hundred research scholars worked on missile-related problems in the laboratories of their respective institutes. The quality of work achieved through this partnership gave me tremendous confidence.

Between April–June 1984, six of us in the missile programme visited campuses and enlisted promising young graduates. We presented an outline of the missile programme before the professors and aspiring students and requested them to participate in the programme. We were expecting around 300 young engineers to join our laboratories.

When India carried out its first nuclear explosion in 1974, we declared ourselves the sixth country in the world to explode a nuclear device. When we launched SLV-3, we were the fifth country to achieve satellite launch capability. When were we going to be the first or second country in the world to achieve a technological feat?

We were working on the action plan that had emerged from a review, when the news of Prime Minister Indira Gandhi's assassination broke. This was followed by the news of widespread violence and riots. A curfew had been imposed in Hyderabad city. We rolled up the PERT charts and a city map was spread out over the table to organise transport and safe passage for all employees. In less than an hour, the laboratory wore a deserted look. I was left sitting alone in my office.

Mrs. Gandhi's death was a tremendous loss to the scientific community. She had given an impetus to scientific research in the country. When her son, Rajiv Gandhi, took over as the new prime minister, he was able to carry forward the policies of his mother—the integrated guided missile development programme being a part of them.

By the summer of 1985, all the groundwork had been completed for building the Missile Technology Research Centre at Imarat Kancha. The young prime minister laid the foundation stone of Research Centre Imarat (RCI) on 3 August 1985. He appeared very pleased with the progress made. He told the DRDL team that he understood the hardships faced by Indian scientists. He expressed his gratitude towards those who preferred to stay in India and work here, despite the odds, rather than go abroad for comfortable careers.

❋ ❋ ❋

The young engineers we had recruited changed the dynamics of DRDL. It was a valuable experience for all of us. When we first assigned these tasks to the young scientists, they did not fully grasp the importance of their work. Once they did, they felt the burden of the tremendous faith placed in them.

I remember one young man telling me, "There is no big shot in our team, how will we be able to break through?"

I told him, "A big shot is a little shot who keeps on shooting, so keep trying!"

It was astonishing to see how, in the young scientific environment, negative attitudes changed to positive, and things that were previously thought impractical began happening. Many older scientists were rejuvenated simply by being part of a young team.

At the review meetings, I would insist that the youngest scientists present their team's work. That would help them visualise the whole system. Gradually, an atmosphere of confidence grew. Young scientists started questioning senior colleagues on solid technical issues. The work environment was lively, with a good blend of the experience of the older scientists and the innovation of their younger colleagues. This positive dependence between youth and experience had created a very productive work culture at DRDL.

The first launch of the missile programme was conducted on 16 September 1985, when *Trishul* successfully took off from the test range at Sriharikota. This was followed by the successful test flight of the pilotless target aircraft (PTA). This was a small but significant step towards developing missile hardware that is not only functional but also acceptable to the user agencies. We were slowly graduating from single-laboratory projects to multi-laboratory programmes and then to laboratory-industry exercises, since a private sector firm was to produce them. We had reached the highway to national self-reliance in missile technology.

I have always had a deep regard for academic institutoins. Taking our partnership with the academic institutions of the country a step further, joint advanced technology programmes were started at the Indian Institute of Science (IISc) and Jadavpur University.

Prithvi had young graduates from Jadavpur University working on it. At the IISc, postgraduate students under the leadership of Prof. IG Sharma developed air defence software for multi-target acquisition by *Akash*. The re-entry vehicle system design methodology for *Agni* was developed by a young team at IIT, Madras, with DRDO scientists. Osmania University's Navigational Electronics Research and Training Unit had developed state-of-the-art signal processing algorithms for *Nag*.

I have only given a few examples of collaborative endeavour. In fact, it would have been very difficult to achieve our advanced technological goals without the active partnership of these academic institutions.

One challenge involved in the *Agni* payload design was related to the tremendous speed with which it would re-enter the atmosphere. (12 times the speed of sound, or 12 Mach) At this tremendous speed, we had no experience of how to keep the vehicle under control. We could not carry out a test, as we had no wind tunnel to generate that kind of speed. If we sought American help, we would have been seen as aspiring to something they considered their exclusive privilege. Even if they consented to co-operate, they would be certain to quote a price for their wind tunnel which was way beyond our entire project budget. The question was how to beat the system.

Prof. SM Deshpande of the IISc found four bright, young scientists working in the field of fluid dynamics who developed the software within six months!

20.   About Motivation and Working Well

As work on the project spread horizontally, performance appraisals for nearly 500 scientists became more and more difficult. DRDO has an assessment-linked policy and I had to write annual confidential reports. These reports would be forwarded to an assessment board (comprised of outside specialists) for recommendations. Many people viewed this part of my job uncharitably. Missing a promotion was conveniently translated as a dislike I had towards them. Promotions of other colleagues were seen as favours granted by me. Entrusted with the task of performance evaluation, I had to be a fair judge.

It is difficult for an individual to objectively judge her or his own actions, which may be, and often are, contradictory to one's good intentions. Most people come to work with the intention of doing that work. Many of them do their work in a manner they find convenient, and leave for home in the evening with a sense of satisfaction. They do not evaluate their performance, only their intentions. They also assume that because they have worked with the intention of finishing in time, any delay caused is due to reasons beyond control. But if one's action or inaction caused that delay, was it not intentional?

Looking back on my days as a young scientist, I am aware that one of the most constant and powerful urges I experienced was my desire to be more than what I was at that moment. I desired to feel more, learn more, express more. I desired to grow, improve and expand. I never used anybody's influence to advance my career. All I had was the inner urge to seek more within myself. The key to my motivation has always been to look at how far I had still to go, rather than how far I had come.

✼ ✼ ✼

I had first attempted to build up a supportive work environment in 1983, while launching IGMDP. The projects were in the design phase at that time. That had resulted in a forty to fifty per cent increase in the level of activity. Now that multiple projects were entering into development and flight-testing stage, I felt it was time for a re-organisation.

The 1983 organisation was done with the objective of renewal— it was indeed a very complex exercise handled deftly by AV Ranga Rao and Col. R Swaminathan. We created a team of new scientists with just one experienced person and gave them several work challenges. These exercises were being attempted for the first time in the country, and the technology involved was comparable with world-class systems. The effort of these young teams (the average age had come down to 33 years from 42 years) made the country self-reliant in the area of protected technologies. It was a good demonstration of the 'renewal factor'. Our intellectual capacity was renewed through contact with enthusiastic young minds.

Now, besides the renewal of manpower, emphasis had to be laid on strengthening the project groups.

21. EARTH TO FIRE: *PRITHVI* TO *AGNI*

Work on *Prithvi* was nearing completion when we entered 1988. The importance of these rocket engines was not restricted to the *Prithvi* project alone—it was a national achievement.

Since the interim test range at Balasore was still at least a year away from completion, we set up special facilities at SHAR for the launch of *Prithvi*. These included a launch pad, block house, control consoles and mobile telemetry stations. I was happily reunited with my old friend MR Kurup who was director of SHAR by then. Working with Kurup on the *Prithvi* launch campaign gave me great satisfaction. He worked for *Prithvi* as a team member—ignoring the boundary lines that divided DRDO and ISRO, DRDL and SHAR. Kurup used to spend a lot of time with us at the launch pad. He complemented us with his experience in range testing and range safety.

Prithvi was launched at 1123 hrs on 25 February 1988. It was an epoch-making event in the history of rocketry in the country. The accuracy of a missile is expressed in terms of its circular error probable (CEP). This measures the radius of a circle within which 50 per cent of the missiles fired will impact. In other words, if a missile has a CEP of 1 km (such as the Iraqi *Scud* missiles fired in the Gulf War), this means that half of them should impact within 1 km of their target. We stressed upon building competence in core guidance and control technologies to achieve a CEP as precise as 50 m.

The launch of *Prithvi* sent shock waves across the neighbouring countries. The response of the West was shock, and then anger. A seven-nation technology embargo was clamped, making it impossible for India to buy anything even remotely connected with the development of guided missiles. The emergence of India as a self-reliant country in the field of guided missiles upset all the developed nations of the world.

Indian core competence in rocketry has been firmly established beyond any doubt. The robust civilian space industry and viable missile-based defences has taken India into a select club of nations.

But would a *Prithvi* suffice? Would the indigenous development of four or five missile systems make us sufficiently strong? Or would having nuclear weapons make us stronger? Missiles and atomic weapons are merely parts of a greater whole. As I saw it, the development of *Prithvi* represented the self-reliance of our country in the field of advanced technology. High technology is synonymous with huge amounts of money and massive infrastructure. Neither of these was available, unfortunately, in adequate measure. So what could we do? Perhaps the *Agni* missile being developed as a technology demonstrator project, pooling all the resources available in the country, was the answer.

I was very sure, even when we had discussed REX in ISRO about a decade earlier, that Indian scientists and technologists working together had the capability to achieve this technological breakthrough. India can most certainly achieve state-of-the-art technology with the combined efforts of its scientific laboratories and academic institutions.

The *Agni* team had more than 500 scientists, and many organisations were networked to undertake this huge launch.

The *Agni* launch had been scheduled for 20 April 1989. This was going to be an unprecedented exercise. Unlike space launch vehicles, a missile launch involves wide-ranging safety hazards. Two radars, three telemetry stations, one telecommand station and four electro-optical tracking instruments had been deployed. The telemetry station at Car Nicobar (ISTRAC) and the SHAR radars were commissioned to track the vehicle. Dynamic surveillance was employed.

All activities preparatory to the launch went according to schedule. We had decided to move the people living in nearby villages to safety at the time of the launch. This attracted media attention, and led to much controversy. By the time 20 April 1989 arrived, the whole nation was watching us. Foreign pressure was exerted through diplomatic channels to abort the flight trial, but the central government staved off any distraction to our work.

We were at T-14 seconds when the computer signalled that one of the instruments was functioning erratically. This was immediately rectified. Meanwhile, the down-range station asked for a 'hold'. In another few seconds, multiple holds were necessitated. We had to abort the launch.

I went to meet my team members, who were in a state of shock and sorrow. I shared my SLV-3 experience with them, "I lost my launch vehicle in the sea, but recovered successfully. Your missile is still in front of you. In fact you have lost nothing that a few weeks of work will not correct." This shook them out of their immobility and the entire team went back to retrieve the subsystems and re-charge them.

The press was up in arms, and fielded various interpretations of the postponement of the flight. Cartoonist Sudhir Dar sketched a shopkeeper returning a product to a salesman saying that like *Agni* it would not take off. Another cartoonist showed one *Agni* scientist explaining that the launch was postponed because the press button did not make contact. The *Hindustan Times* showed a leader consoling press reporters, "There's no need for any alarm...it's a purely peaceful, non-violent missile."

After a detailed analysis conducted virtually around the clock for the next ten days, our scientists had the missile ready for launch on 1 May 1989. But, again, during the automatic computer checkout period at T-10 seconds, a hold signal was indicated. The launch had to be postponed yet again!

Now, such things are very common in rocketry and happen quite often in other countries too. But the expectant nation was in no mood to appreciate our difficulties. *The Hindu* carried a cartoon by Keshav showing a villager counting some currency notes and commenting to another, "Yes, it's the compensation for moving away from my hut near the test site—a few more postponements and I can build a house of my own..." Another cartoonist designated *Agni* as "IDBM—Intermittently Delayed Ballistic Missile." *Amul's* cartoon suggested that what *Agni* needed to do was use their butter as fuel!

I spoke to the DRDL–RCI community, at a gathering of more than 2,000 persons. "Very rarely is a laboratory or an R&D establishment given an opportunity to be the first in the country to develop a system such as *Agni*. A great opportunity has been given to us. Naturally major opportunities are accompanied by equally major challenges. We should not give up. We should not allow the problem to defeat us. The country doesn't deserve anything less than success from us. Let us aim for success." I had almost completed my address, when I found myself telling my people, "I promise you, we will be back after successfully launching *Agni* before the end of this month."

It was nothing short of amazing how hundreds of scientists and staff worked continuously and completed the system readiness, with acceptance tests, in just 10 days. But now it was the turn of hostile weather conditions to create impediments. A cyclone threat was looming large. All the work centres were connected through satellite communication—meteorological data became intermittent and started flowing in at ten-minute intervals.

Finally, the launch was scheduled for 22 May 1989. The night before, Dr. Arunachalam, Gen. KN Singh and I went walking with Defence Minister KC Pant, who had come to ITR to witness the launch. It was a full-moon night and the high tide caused the waves to crash and roar. Would we succeed with the *Agni* launch tomorrow? This question was uppermost in our minds, but none of us was willing to break the spell cast by the beautiful night.

Breaking a long silence, the defence minister finally asked me, "Kalam! what would you like me to do to celebrate *Agni's* success tomorrow?"

It was a simple question, to which I could not think of an answer immediately. What did I want? What was it that I did not have? What could make me happier? And then I found the answer. "We need 100,000 saplings to plant at RCI," I said.

22.   THE FIRE OF SUCCESS: RECOGNITION AND LOVE

The next day *Agni* took off at 0710 hrs. It was a perfect launch. The missile followed a textbook trajectory. All flight parameters were met. It was like waking up to a beautiful morning after a nightmarish sleep. We had reached the launch pad after five years of continuous work at multiple work centres. We had lived through the ordeal of a series of snags in the last five weeks. We had survived pressure from everywhere to stop the programme. But we had done it, at last!

It was one of the greatest moments of my life. A mere 600 seconds of elegant flight washed off our fatigue in an instant. What a wonderful way to culminate the years of labour!

I wrote in my diary that night,

> Do not look at *Agni*
> as an entity directed upward,
> to deter the ominous
> or exhibit your might.
> It is a fire
> in the heart of an Indian.
> Do not even give it
> the form of a missile,
> as it clings to the
> burning pride of this nation
> and thus is bright.

Prime Minister Rajiv Gandhi called the *Agni* launch "a major achievement in our continuing efforts to safeguard our independence and security by self-reliant means."

President R Venkataraman saw in the *Agni* success the fulfilment of his dream. He cabled me from Simla, "It is a tribute to your dedication, hard work, and talent."

✳ ✳ ✳

A great deal of misinformation and rumours had been spread by vested interests about this mission. *Agni* had never been intended only as a nuclear weapon system. What it did was to afford us the option of developing the ability to deliver non-nuclear weapons with high precision, at long ranges. It provided us with a viable non-nuclear option.

Great ire was raised by the test firing of *Agni*, especially in the USA, where Congressmen threatened to put a stop to all missile-related technologies, along with all multi-national aid.

Gary Mulhollin, a so-called specialist in missiles and warhead technologies, had made a claim in *The Wall Street Journal* that India had made *Agni* with the help of West Germany (now Germany). An immediate denial came from the West Germans, who in turn speculated that France had supplied the *Agni* guidance electronics.

American Senator Jeff Bingaman even went to the extent of suggesting that I picked up everything needed for *Agni* during my four-month stay in Virginia in 1962. The fact that I was in Virginia more than 25 years ago—at that time the technology used in *Agni* did not exist, even in the USA—was not mentioned.

In today's world, technological backwardness leads to the threat of subjugation. Can we allow our freedom to be compromised on this account? It is our duty to guarantee the security and integrity of our nation against this threat.

Agni marked the completion of five years of IGMDP. With tactical missiles like *Prithvi* and *Trishul* already test fired, the launches of *Nag* and *Akash* would take us into areas of competence where there is little or no international competition. There was a need to focus our efforts more intensively on them.

In September 1989, I was invited by the Maharashtra Academy of Sciences in Bombay to deliver the Jawaharlal Nehru Memorial Lecture. I used this opportunity to share with the budding scientists my plans of making an indigenous air-to-air missile, *Astra*, to follow the development of the Indian light combat aircraft (LCA).

The second flight of *Prithvi* at the end of September 1988 was again a great success. *Prithvi* has proved to be the best surface-to-surface missile in the world today. It can carry 1,000 kg of warhead to a distance of 250 km and deliver it within a radius of 50 metres. It is one hundred per cent indigenous in all respects—design, operations and deployment. It can be produced in large numbers as the production facilities in BDL were built during the development phase itself. The army was quick to recognise the potential and soon placed orders for *Prithvi* and *Trishul* missile systems, something that had never happened before.

In 1990, on Republic Day, the nation celebrated the success of its missile programme. I was conferred the Padma Vibhushan along with Dr. Arunachalam. Two of my other colleagues— JC Bhattacharya and RN Agarwal—were also decorated with Padma Shree awards. It was the first time in the history of free India that so many scientists affiliated to the same organisation found their names on the awards list.

Memories of the Padma Bhushan awarded a decade ago came alive. I still lived more or less as I had lived then—in a room ten feet wide and twelve feet long, furnished mainly with books, papers and a few pieces of hired furniture. The only difference was that at that time, my room was in Trivandrum and now it was in Hyderabad.

I was touched by the recognition bestowed on me by my country. A large number of scientists and engineers leave this country at the first opportunity to earn more money abroad. It is true that they definitely get greater monetary benefits, but could anything compensate for this love and respect from one's own countryfolk?

I sat alone for a while in silent contemplation. The sand and shells of Rameswaram, the care of Iyadurai Solomon in Ramanathapuram, the guidance of Rev. Father Sequeira in Trichy and Prof. Pandalai in Madras, the encouragement of Dr. Mediratta in Bangalore, the hovercraft ride with Prof. Menon, the pre-dawn visit to the Tilpat Range with Prof. Sarabhai, the healing touch of Dr. Brahm Prakash on the day of SLV-3's failure, the national jubilation on the launch of SLV-3, Mrs. Gandhi's appreciative smile, the post-SLV-3 simmering at VSSC, Prof. Ramanna's faith in inviting me to DRDO, the IGMDP, the creation of RCI, Prithvi, Agni...a flood of memories swept over me. I wished I could meet all of them and share my joy.

❋ ❋ ❋

A fortnight later, NR Iyer and his team celebrated the awards for the missile programme with the maiden flight of *Nag*. They repeated the feat again on the very next day.

India had thus achieved the status of having a third generation anti-tank missile system with 'fire-and-forget' capability—on par with any state-of-the-art technology in the world. Indigenous composite technology had achieved a major milestone—and proven that innovation cannot be suppressed by international restrictions.

❋ ❋ ❋

I went to Madurai Kamaraj University the same month to deliver their convocation address. When I reached Madurai, I asked after my high school teacher Iyadurai Solomon, who was by now a Reverend and eighty years old. I was told that he lived in a suburb of Madurai. I took a taxi and went looking for his house. Rev. Solomon knew that I was going to give the convocation address that day, but had no way of getting there. That made me all the more glad that I could meet him and bring him to the convocation. It was a touching meeting between teacher and pupil. Dr. PC Alexander, the governor of Tamilnadu, who was presiding over the function, was deeply moved on seeing the elderly teacher and requested him to share the dais with us.

"The convocation day of every university is like opening the floodgates of energy, an energy that, when harnessed by institutions, organisations and industry, aids in nation-building,"

I told the young graduates. Somehow I felt I was echoing Rev. Solomon's words, spoken about half a century ago. After that lecture, I bowed down before my teacher.

"You have not only reached my goals, Kalam. You have eclipsed them!," he told me in a voice choked with emotion.

The next month, I happened to be in Trichy and used that opportunity to visit St. Joseph's College. I did not find Rev. Father Sequeira or any of my old teachers there, but it seemed to me that the stones of the college building still carried the wisdom of those great people. I shared with the young students my memories at St. Joseph's and paid tribute to the teachers who had moulded me.

Towards the end of 1990, Jadavpur University conferred on me the honour of Doctor of Science at a special convocation. I was a little embarrassed at finding my name mentioned along with that of the legendary Nelson Mandela, who was also honoured at the same convocation. What could I possible have in common with a legend like Mandela? The only common factor seemed to be our persistence in our missions.

My mission of advancing rocketry in my country was perhaps nothing when compared with Mandela's mission to achieve dignity and the right to equality for his Coloured compatriots; but there was no difference in the intensity of our passions.

※ ※ ※

We celebrated the nation's forty-fourth Independence Day with the test firing of *Akash*. The country had taken an important step in ground-based air defence. The Missile Council (MC) declared 1991 the Year of Initiative for DRDL and RCI.

Rear Admiral Mohan, who had been in charge of *Trishul*, retired. I had always admired Mohan's understanding of missile command guidance. This sailor-teacher-scientist could outwit any other expert in the country in this field. I remember his candid exposition of various aspects of the guidance system during the *Trishul* meetings. Once, he showed me a verse that he had composed to highlight the woes of an IGMDP project director. It was a good way of letting off steam,

> Impossible timeframes, PERT charts to boot
> Are driving me almost crazy as a coot.
> Presentations to MC add to one's woes,
> If they solve anything, heaven only knows.
> Meetings on holidays, even at night,
> The family is fed up, and all ready for flight.
> My hands are itching to tear my hair—
> But alas! I haven't any more to tear!

I told him, "I have handed over all my problems to my best teams in DRDL, RCI and other participating labs. That has given me a full head of hair!"

✳ ✳ ✳

The year 1991 had begun on a very ominous note. On the night of 15 January 1991, the Gulf War broke out between Iraq and the Allied forces led by the USA. In one stroke, thanks to satellite television invading Indian skies by that time, the rockets and missiles captured the imagination of the entire nation. People started discussing *Scuds* and *Patriots* in coffeehouses and teashops. Children began flying paper kites shaped like missiles, and playing war games along the lines of what they saw on American television networks. The successful test firing of *Prithvi* and *Trishul* during the course of the Gulf War was enough to make an anxious nation relax.

The nation was quick to draw parallels between the missiles operational in the Gulf War and our own warhead. A common query I encountered was whether *Prithvi* was superior to a *Scud*, whether *Akash* could perform like a *Patriot*, and so on. On hearing a "Yes" or a "Why not?" from me, people's faces would light up with pride and satisfaction.

The Allied forces had a marked technological edge, as they were fielding systems built using the technologies of the eighties and nineties. Iraq was fighting with the by-and-large vintage weapon system of the sixties and seventies.

Now, this is where the key to the modern world order lies—superiority through technology. Deprive the opponent of the latest technology and then dictate your terms in an unequal contest. The Chinese war philosopher, Sun Tzu, said over 2000 years ago, "What matters in war is not decimating the enemy army physically, but breaking the ememy's will so as to make it concede defeat in the mind." He seems to have predicted the domination of technology in the twentieth-century theatres of war. Electronic warfare, and not guerrilla combat, has come to dominate the politics of war in the twenty-first century—with missiles and electronic and information warfare playing the lead roles.

The term technology, for many people, conjures up images of smoky steel mills and clanking machines. This is a rather inadequate conception of what technology denotes. The invention of the horse collar in the Middle Ages led to major changes in agricultural methods, and was as much a technological advance as the invention of the Bessemer furnace some centuries later. Technology includes the techniques as well as the machines that may be necessary to apply these techniques. In fact, technology includes ways to make chemical reactions occur, ways to breed fish, eradicate weeds, light up theatres, treat patients, to fight wars—and, even more importantly, to prevent them.

Today, most advanced technological processes—especially in electronics and space technology—are carried out in relative silence. Clean surroundings are characteristic, even essential.

The assembly line—with the long lines of people carrying out simple, routine functions—is an anachronism. Our symbols of technology must therefore change before we can keep pace with changes in technology itself.

We should never forget that technology feeds on itself. Helpful technology makes more technology possible. In fact, technological innovation consists of three stages linked together in a self-reinforcing cycle. First, there is the creative stage—the blueprint of a feasible idea. This is made real by its practical application, which is the second stage. The third and final stage is its diffusion through society—where its worth is measured. The process is then complete; the loop is closed.

After the Gulf War concluded with the victory of the technologically superior Allied forces, over 500 scientists of DRDL and RCI gathered to discuss the issues that had emerged. The discussion led to many more serious questions, such as, how to establish effective electronic warfare support? How to make missile development proceed alongside the development of equally necessary systems like the LCA? What were the key areas where a push would bring progress?

At the end of a lively discussion spread over three hours, the general conclusion was that it was necessary to have the same capability in specific areas as your potential opponent. The scientists vowed to achieve all this for of *Prithvi*, *Trishul* and *Agni* by the end of the year. The vow was later fulfilled. That year also saw the tube-launched *Nag* flights, and the manoeuvre of *Trishul* at seven metres above sea level, at speeds which exceeded three times the speed of sound.

The same year, I received an honorary degree of Doctor of Science from IIT, Bombay. In the citation read by Prof. B Nag on the occasion, I was described as "an inspiration behind the creation of a solid technological base from which India's future aerospace programmes can be launched to meet the challenges of the twenty-first century."

I do believe that India will enter the next century with its own satellite in geo-stationary orbit 36,000 km away in space, positioned by its own launch vehicle. India will also become a missile power. Ours is a country with tremendous vitality. Even though the world may not see its full potential or feel its full power, no one can dare ignore it any more.

＊ ＊ ＊

On 15 October 1991, I turned sixty. I looked forward to retirement and planned to open a school for less-privileged children. My friend, Prof. P Rama Rao, who was then heading the Department of Science and Technology in the Government of India, even struck up a partnership with me to establish what he called the Rao–Kalam school. We both believed that our achievements, however impressive they might appear to be, were not all there is to life. But we had to postpone our plan as neither of us was relieved from our posts by the government.

23. SHARING INSIGHTS

It was during this period that I decided to write my memoirs and express my observations and opinions on certain issues.

The biggest problem faced in one's youth is the lack of clarity of vision, a lack of direction. It was then that I decided to write about the circumstances and people who made me what I am today. The idea was not merely to pay tribute to some individuals or highlight certain aspects of my life. What I wanted to say was that no one—however poor or underprivileged—need feel disheartened. Problems are a part of life. Suffering is the essence of success. As someone said:

God has not promised
Skies always blue,
Flower-strewn pathways
All our life through.

God has not promised
Sun without rain,
Joy without sorrow
Peace without pain.

But God has promised
Strength for the day,
Rest for the labour
Light for the way.

I will not be presumptuous enough to say that my life can be a role model for anybody; but some child living in an obscure place, in an underprivileged social setting, may find a little solace in the way my destiny has been shaped. It could perhaps help such children liberate themselves from the bondage of their imagined backwardness and hopelessness. Irrespective of where they are right now, they should be aware that God is with them, and in that case who can be against them?

I have worked with many people and organisations—having to deal with people who were so full of their own limitations that they had no way to prove their self-worth other than by intimidating me.

Technology, unlike science, is a group activity. It is not based on individual intelligence, but on the interacting intelligence of many. I think the biggest success of IGMDP is not the fact that the country acquired the capability of making five state-of-the-art missile systems in record time, but that through it, a few superb teams of scientists and engineers were created. If someone asks me about my personal achievements in Indian rocketry, I would pin it down to having created an environment in which teams of young people could put their heart and soul into their missions.

When we first began creating project teams during SLV-3, and later in IGMDP, the people working in these teams found themselves in the frontline of their organisations' ambitions. As such, the members became both highly visible and highly vulnerable. They were personally expected to make disproportionate contributions to win collective glory.

In the early years of the SLV-3 project, I often had to deal with nervousness at the top because progress was not immediately visible. Many felt that the organisation had lost control over SLV-3, that the team would run on unchecked, causing chaos and confusion. But on all occasions, these fears were proved imaginary.

The SLV-3 team developed their own internal success criteria. We laid down our own standards, expectations and objectives. We had our own way of summarising what needed to happen for us to be successful and how we would measure success. Some of these criteria were—how were we going to accomplish our tasks, who would do what and to what standards, what were the time limits, and how would the team conduct itself with reference to others in the organisation?

The process of arriving at the success criteria within a team is an intricate and skilled one because there is a lot happening under the surface. On the surface, the team is simply pushing activities to achieve the project's mission goals. But I have repeatedly seen how people are not too good at stating what they want—until they see a work centre doing something they don't want them to do. A project team member must in fact act like a detective. She or he should probe for clues on how the project is proceeding, and then put together different bits of evidence to build up a clear and deep understanding of the project's needs and requirements.

24.　LOOKING AHEAD

Mahatma Gandhi emphasised grassroots technology and put the customer at the centre of the entire business activity. JRD Tata brought in progress-driven infrastructure. Dr. Homi Jehangir Bhabha and Prof. Vikaram Sarabhai launched the high technology-based atomic energy and space programmes.

Advancing the developmental philosophy of Dr. Bhabha and Prof. Sarabhai, Dr. MS Swaminathan ushered the Green Revolution into India. Dr. Verghese Kurien brought in a powerful co-operative movement through a revolution in the dairy industry. Prof. Satish Dhawan developed mission management concepts in space research.

With IGMDP, I attempted to integrate the vision of Prof. Sarabhai and the mission of Prof. Dhawan by adapting the high-technology setting of Dr. Brahm Prakash's space research. I tried to create a completely indigenous variety of technology management.

In 1983, we did not have an adequate technology base. A few pockets of expertise were available, but we lacked the empowerment to utilise that expert technology. We attempted to develop a model that was appropriate, even tailor-made, for our very specific needs and capabilities. We borrowed ideas that had been developed elsewhere, but adapted them in the light of what we knew were our strengths, at the same time recognising the constraints we would be compelled to work under. All in all, appropriate management helped to prove what talent and potential lay in our research laboratories, government institutions and private industries.

The Technology Management philosophy of the missile development programme is not exclusive to missile development. It represents the urge to succeed and an awareness that the world is never again to be directed by muscle- or money-power. Only nations with technological superiority will enjoy freedom and sovereignty.

And, as I said in the beginning, technology, unlike science, is a group activity. It does not grow on individual intelligence, but by intelligences interacting and ceaselessly influencing one another. And that is what I tried to make IGMDP—a strong Indian family, which also makes missile systems.

There has been much speculation and philosophising about the life and times of our scientists, but not enough exploration in determining where they wanted to go and how they reached there. In sharing with you the story of my struggle to become a person, I have perhaps tried to give you some insight into this journey. I hope it will equip at least a few young people to stand up in our society. People tend to get addicted to the endless pursuit of external rewards—wealth, prestige, position, promotion, approval of one's lifestyle by others, ceremonial honours and status symbols of all kinds.

The youth of today must de-learn this self-defeating way of living. The culture of working for material possessions and rewards must be discarded.

When I see wealthy, powerful, learned people struggling to be at peace with themselves, I remember people like Ahmed Jallaluddin and Iyadurai Solomon. How happy they were with virtually no possessions!

How did they feel so secure without anything to fall back upon?

I believe they drew sustenance from within. They relied more on the inner signals and less on the external markers that I have mentioned above.

Take this from me, the more decisions you can make avoiding external pressures—which will constantly try to manipulate and immobilise you—the better your life will be. The entire nation will benefit by having strong, inner-directed people as its citizens.

Your willingness to use your own inner resources, especially your imagination, will bring you success. When you undertake a task from your own uniquely individual standpoint, you will become a person.

You, me, everyone on this planet is sent by God with the freedom to cultivate all the creative potential within us. We differ in the way we make our choices and evolve our destiny. Life is a difficult game. You have to be willing to ignore the pressure to do things the way others say they should be done.

What will you call Sivasubramania Iyer inviting me to have lunch in his kitchen? Zohara mortgaging her gold bangles and chains to get me into engineering college? Prof. Sponder insisting that I should sit with him in the front row for the group photograph? Making a hovercraft in a motor garage set-up? Dr. Brahm Prakash's support? Capt. Narayanan's management? R Venkataraman's vision? Dr. Arunachalam's drive? Each is an example of a strong inner strength and initiative.

I am not a philosopher. I am only a man of technology. I have spent all my life learning rocketry. But, working with a very large cross-section of people in different organisations, I have had an opportunity to understand the phenomenon of professional life in its bewildering complexity.

When you look down from an aircraft, people, houses, rocks, fields, trees, all appear as one homogeneous landscape, very difficult to

Plate 13

The successful launch of *Prithvi*, the surface-to-surface weapons system.

Plate 14

One of the cartoons printed in the newspapers after the failure of the first two *Agni* launches.

Plate 15

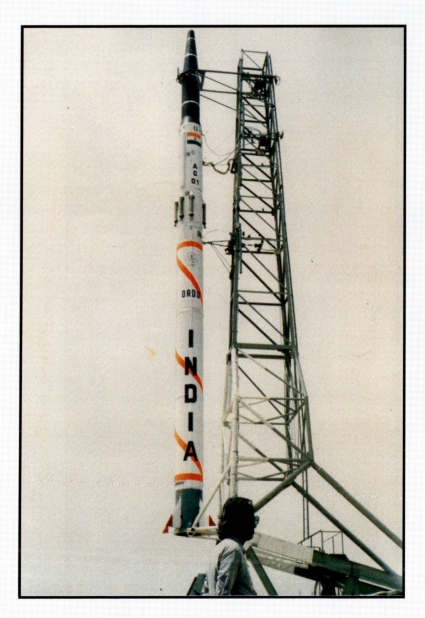

A long-cherished dream; *Agni* on the launch pad.

Plate 16

Being carried by a jubilant crowd after the successful launch of *Agni.*

Plate 17

With the three Service Chiefs. To my left is Admiral VS Shekhawat; on my right are General BC Joshi and Air Chief Marshall SK Kaul.

Plate 18

Recieiving the Bharat Ratna from President KR Narayanan.

Plate 19

Pokhran-II: aerial image of one of the subsidence craters at the site of the nuclear tests.

With Rajagopala Chidambaram at a press conference following the Pokhran tests.

Plate 20

With students at Rashtrapati Bhavan.

distinguish from one another. What you have just read is a similar bird's-eye view of my life, seen, as it were, from afar.

My colleagues, associates, leaders are the real heroes of the drama I lived. The complex science of rocketry, the important issues of technology management, all seem to have been treated in a diagrammatic manner. The pain and cheer, the achievements and the failures all appear grouped together.

This is the story of the period ending with the first *Agni* launch. It is the story of the son of Jainulabdeen, who lived for over a hundred years in Rameswaram and died there; the story of a lad who sold newspapers to help his brother; the story of a pupil reared by Sivasubramania Iyer and Iyadurai Solomon; the story of a student taught by inspired teachers; the story of an engineer spotted by MGK Menon and groomed by the legendary Prof. Sarabhai; the story of a scientist tested by failures and setbacks; the story of a leader supported by a large team of brilliant and dedicated professionals.

This story will end with me, for I have no inheritance in the worldly sense. I have acquired nothing, built nothing, possess nothing— no family, sons or daughters.

AFTERWORD

After the success of the integrated guided missile development programme, Dr. APJ Abdul Kalam served as scientific adviser to the defence minister, and as head of the Defence Research and Development Organisation. During this period, he was closely involved with Operation Shakti, the Pokhran-II nuclear tests that were conducted in May 1998, in collaboration with the Department of Atomic Energy. But, the path to Pokhran-II had not been easy.

The nuclear Non-Proliferation Treaty (NPT) had been first drafted in 1968. In May 1974, India tested its nuclear explosives in Pokhran for the first time, facing severe international criticism after the tests. The NPT steadily gained supporters over the years, and by the mid-90s, the vast majority of nations in the world had signed it. (By the year 2000, only four nations out of 191 had not signed the treaty, India being one of the four.) India had endorsed the NPT in principle, but refrained from signing it because of objections to legitimate 'nuclear power' status that was granted to five nations—the USA, UK, Russia (then USSR), France and China. India agreed to sign the NPT if these nations committed themselves to a specific time-table to achieve nuclear disarmament, an approach the five nations refused to consider.

Instead, the nuclear powers formulated two treaties that would restrict nuclear tests—the Comprehensive Test Ban Treaty (CTBT) to prohibit all nuclear tests, and the Fissile Material Cut-off Treaty (FMCT) to cut off production of fissile materials for weapons. Neither of these treaties would put the five nations, who already possessed large stockpiles of tested weapons, through any serious inconvenience.

India was put under intense pressure, particularly from the USA, to sign the two treaties. The new international demand was to limit the spread of nuclear weapons, but not to reduce those already held by the major powers. It was in this political climate that the Indian government decided to come out of hiding and test its nuclear weapons.

In May 1998, amidst heavy secrecy, India tested its nuclear devices at Pokhran, twenty-four years after the first nuclear tests were conducted at the same site. A couple of weeks later, in retaliation to the Indian tests, Pakistan tested its nuclear devices at Chagai hills. The tests caused fear of a nuclear arms race in the subcontinent.

With the success of Pokhran-II, Dr. Kalam became a heroic figure for many Indians. From November 1999 to November 2001, he served as principal scientific adviser to the Government of India, in the rank of a cabinet minister. He was responsible for evolving policies, strategies and missions for many development applications. As chairman of the Technology Information, Forecasting and Assessment Council (TIFAC), he formulated Technology Vision 2020, on outline that he believed would take India from its present status as a developing nation to that of a developed nation.

Dr. Kalam had been previously awarded the Padma Bhushan in 1981, the Padma Vibhushan in 1990, and the highest civilian award in India, the Bharat Ratna, in 1997.

Towards the end of 2001, Dr. Kalam returned to academic pursuit. He took over as professor of technology and societal transformation at Anna University, Chennai.

In 2002, he was nominated by the ruling political party to the post of President of the Indian Republic. It is testimony to his popularity that he was elected with little opposition. On 25 July 2002, Dr. Kalam was sworn in as the eleventh President of India.

People who Influenced Dr A P J Abdul Kalam

The Early Years

Ahmed Jallaluddin, a close friend and mentor. He would later become Dr Kalam's brother-in-law, when he married Zohara, Dr Kalam's sister.

Iyadurai Solomon, Dr Kalam's teacher at Schwartz High School, Ramanathapuram; he urged his students to challenge their destiny and instilled in Dr Kalam the power of faith.

Jainulabdeen, Dr Kalam's father, who passed away in 1976, at the age of 102.

Professor KAV Pandalai, professor of aerostructure design and analysis at MIT; a man of great intellectual integrity and scholarship, and a friendly and enthusiastic teacher.

Professor Narasingha Rao, professor of theoretical aerodynamics at MIT, whose keen method of teaching made Dr Kalam prefer mathematical physics to any other subject.

Professor Sponder, professor of technical aerodynamics at MIT, who taught Dr Kalam that one must have aptitude and passion for one's chosen field of study.

Ramakrishna Iyer, Dr Kalam's mathematics teacher at Schwartz High School, Ramanathapuram.

Samsuddin, another close friend and mentor; he ran a newspaper agency in Rameswaram and gave Dr Kalam his first job.

Sivasubramania Iyer, Dr Kalam's science teacher in Rameswaram Elementary School. Although from an orthodox background himself, he was determined to break some of the social barriers that prevailed in their small town.

The Working Years

Brahm Prakash (d. 1984) was the first Indian to head the Department of Metallurgy in the Indian Institute of Science. He developed techniques for the extraction and fabrication of a variety of nuclear-grade metals. Subsequently, Dr. Brahm Prakash became the first director of the Vikram Sarabhai Space Centre, which oversaw the launch of SLV-3. The geosynchronous satellite launch vehicle (GSLV) was his legacy to the Indian space community.

Homi Jehangir Bhabha (1909–66) is considered the architect of the Indian atomic energy programme. He founded the Tata Institute of Fundamental Research (TIFR) in Mumbai, which became the focal point of the atomic energy programme in its early years. In 1954, he founded the Bhabha Atomic Research

Centre (BARC) in Trombay. He was also the first secretary of the Department of Atomic Energy (DAE).

R Venkatraman (b. 1910) served as minister of state for defence in the Congress government, under Indira Gandhi. He was elected Vice President in August, 1984. In July 1987, he was sworn in as the eighth President of India.

Raja Ramanna (1925–2004) pioneered nuclear physics in India, with his research in nuclear fission. Prof. Ramanna served as director of the Bhabha Atomic Research Centre, chairman of the Indian Atomic Energy Commission, and secretary in the Department of Atomic Energy. In 1974, after he steered India's first nuclear test in Pokhran, he transmitted a coded message to Prime Minister Indira Gandhi which said, "The Buddha is smiling." He was later scientific adviser to the Defence Ministry and elected minister of state for defence in 1990.

Satish Dhawan (1920–2002) helmed the space programme in India after its founder, Vikram Sarabhai, passed away. At the age of 42, Prof. Dhawan became the youngest director of the Indian Institute of Science. He oversaw the building of the first supersonic wind tunnels in the country. He was also chairman of the Space Commission, and president of the Indian Academy of Sciences. In 2002, the launch centre at Sriharikota was renamed the Satish Dhawan Space Centre.

Tipu Sultan (1753–99) was ruler of the kingdom of Mysore from 1782 till his death. He led four major wars against the British East India Company. He was killed in battle in the fourth war and his kingdom was annexed to the Company. One notable military advance championed by Tipu Sultan was the use of rocket brigades in his army.

Vikram Sarabhai (1919–71) was born into an affluent family of industrialists in Ahmedabad. As a research scholar, he worked under Sir CV Raman at the Indian Institute of Science. He was instrumental in setting up the Physical Research Laboratory in Ahmedabad, in 1947. With active support from Homi Bhabha, Prof. Sarabhai set up India's first rocket launching station (TERLS) at Thumba. He was appointed chairman of the Atomic Energy Commission in May 1966. Prof. Sarabhai believed in the practical application of science and its benefits for the common man—like development in communication, meteorology, remote sensing and education. He initiated India's space programme when he undertook the launch of an indigenously built Indian satellite. TERLS was renamed the Vikram Sarabhai Space Centre after his death.

Wernher von Braun (1912–77) was one of the most important rocket scientists and champions of space exploration. Von Braun developed the V-2 ballistic missile for Germany during World War II. For fifteen years after World War II, von Braun worked with the USA in the development of ballistic missiles. In 1960, he became the chief architect of the *Saturn V* launch vehicle, the super booster that would propel the first humans to the moon.

LIST OF ABBREVIATED TERMS

A&ATU	Aircraft and Armament Testing Unit
ADE	Aeronautical Development Establishment
ASLV	Augmented satellite launch vehicle
BARC	Bhabha Atomic Research Centre
BDL	Bharat Dynamics Limited
CCPA	Cabinet Committee for Political Affairs
CEP	Circular error probable
CNES	*Centre Nationale de Etudes Spatiales* (in France)
CPWD	Central Public Works Department
CSIR	Council of Scientific and Industrial Research
CTBT	Comprehensive Test Ban Treaty
DAE	Department of Atomic Energy
DEAL	Defence Electronics Applications Laboratory
DMRL	Defence Metallurgical Research Laboratory
DoS	Department of Space
DRDL	Defence Research and Development Laboratory
DRDO	Defence Research and Development Organisation
DTD&P (Air)	Directorate of Technical Development and Production (Air)
EME	Electronic and Mechanical Engineering (an army corps)
GEM	Ground equipment machine
GMDP	Guided missile development programme
GSLV	Geosynchronous satellite launch vehicle
HAL	Hindustan Aeronautics Limited
IAF	Indian Air Force
IGMDP	Integrated guided missile development programme
IISc	Indian Institute of Science
IIT	Indian Institute of Technology

INCOSPAR	Indian Committee for Space Research
INSA	Indian National Science Academy
IRBM	Intermediate range ballistic missile
ISAS	Institute of Space and Aeronautical Sciences (in Japan)
ISRO	Indian Space Research Organisation
ISTRAC	ISRO Telemetry Tracking and Command Network
ITR	Interim test range
LCA	Light combat aircraft
MES	Military Engineering Services
MIT	Madras Institute of Technology
MoD	Ministry of Defence
MVA	Megavolt ampere
NASA	National Aeronautics and Space Administration (in the USA)
NPL	National Physical Laboratory
NPT	Non-Proliferation Treaty
NRSA	National Remote Sensing Agency
PERT	Programme evaluation and review technique
PRL	Physical Research Laboratory
PSLV	Polar satellite launch vehicle
PTA	Pilotless target aircraft
R&D	Research and development
RATO	Rocket-assisted take-off system
RCI	Research Centre Imarat
REX	Re-entry experiment
RSR	*Rohini* sounding rocket programme
SAM	Surface-to-air missile
SHAR	Sriharikota Rocket Launch Station
SLV	Satellite launching vehicle
SSC	Space Science Council
TERLS	Thumba Equatorial Rocket Launch Station

TIFR	Tata Institute of Fundamental Research
USA	United States of America
USSR	Union of Soviet Socialist Republics (an erstwhile title; in 1991, the USSR collapsed and several new nations were created)
VFR	*Verein fuer Raumschiffahrt* (or Society for Space Flight, in Germany)
VIP	Very important person
VSSC	Vikram Sarabhai Space Centre

GLOSSARY

abort   the act of bringing something to an early end due to a problem or fault

aerodynamics   the study of the interaction between air and solid bodies moving through it

aeronautics   the study of travel through air

Agni   an intermediate-range ballistic missile

Akash   a medium-range surface-to-air missile

algorithms   a set of rules to be followed in calculations

amalgamation   the act of combining or uniting organisations or structures

anti-tank missile   a missile used against enemy tanks

armed forces   a country's army, navy and air force

Arms Race   An arms race is a competition between two or more countries for military supremacy, when each country aims to produce superior numbers of weapons or superior military technology. The term arms race is used generically to describe any competition where there is no absolute goal, only the relative goal of staying ahead of the other competitors. The Arms Race referred to in the book is the one that escalated between the USA and the USSR, after World War II and till the collapse of the USSR in the early 1990s.

ballistic missile   a missile with a high, arching trajectory, which is initially powered and guided, but falls under gravity onto its target

block house   a reinforced concrete shelter used as an observation point

blueprint   a design or technical drawing, which acts as a model or template

bulkhead   a dividing wall between separate compartments in an aircraft, or other vehicle

bureaucratic   to be concerned with complicated administrative procedures

civilian a person not in the armed forces or police forces

closed-circuit TV a television system by which video signals are recorded and transmitted to a restricted set of monitors

collaborative produced or conducted by two or more parties working together

composite materials materials made up of various elements

concentration camp a place where political prisoners or members of persecuted minorities are imprisoned, usually to provide forced labour or to await execution; the term is most strongly associated with the several hundred camps established by the Nazis between 1933–45

control console a panel or unit accommodating a set of controls for equipment

corps a main subdivision of an army, consisting of two or more divisions

cosmos the universe, when seen as a well-ordered whole

countdown counting numerals in reverse order, down to zero; especially before the final moments of a significant event

counter-attack an attack made in response to one made by an opponent

decipher to make out the meaning of something despite it being obscure; to decode

de-commissioned aircraft aircraft that have been withdrawn from service

deploy move into position; used usually for military action

disarmament the action of giving up or deactivating weapons (usually nuclear weapons)

dynamic surveillance continuous and close observation

electro-optical the effect of electrical fields on light and the optical properties of substances

embargo an official ban on trade or other commercial activity with a particular country

exposition comprehensive description and explanation of an idea or theory

fighter plane a fast military aircraft designed for attacking enemy aircraft; *bomber planes* are military aircraft designed to bomb targets in enemy territory

flying hours the time logged by a pilot in flight

guerrilla warfare irregular warfare; when small, independent groups take on larger, organised forces in combat

Gulf War The Gulf War (1990–91) was a conflict between Iraq and a coalition force of 34 nations led by the USA (called the Allied forces). The war started with the Iraqi invasion of Kuwait in August 1990.

hovercraft a vehicle that travels over both land and water, on a cushion of air provided by a downward blast (first patented in 1955)

human centrifuge a piece of equipment that aviation physiologists use, under controlled circumstances, to understand the stress undergone by pilots in terms of G (gravitational force) stresses

indigenous local, (here) made within the country, and not imported

integrated combine more than one thing to make a whole

interface a point of contact, where two systems or organisations meet and interact

jettisonable nose cones discardable nose cones (the cone-shaped nose of an aircraft)

log (of an aircraft or ship) to make a record of something

Mach the ratio of the speed of a body with the speed of sound (used with a numeral, Mach 2 being twice the speed of sound)

Madras State At the time of independence in 1947, Tamilnadu was part of an administrative unit in British India, called Madras Presidency or Madras State. In 1956, the Tamil-speaking areas of Madras Presidency were carved into a separate state called Madras. In 1968, the state was renamed Tamilnadu, with its capital city at Madras (now Chennai).

malfunction (machinery or equipment) failing to function satisfactorily

manoeuvre movement requiring skill and care

missile a weapon that is self-propelled at a target, or directed by remote control, and carries conventional or nuclear explosives

Nag an anti-tank guided missile

Nazi The term Nazi is a short form of the ideology institutionalised in the NSDAP (*Nationalsozialistische Deutsche Arbeiterpartei*), the National Socialist German Workers' Party or Nazi party for short. It lasted in power in Germany for 13 years, from 1933 to 1945. The Nazis sent massive armies to occupy much of continental Europe and endorsed the integration of all people of supposed pure Germanic origin. These invasions set the stage for World War II.

nosedive steep, downward plunge in an aircraft

nuclear weapon A nuclear weapon is a weapon that derives its energy from nuclear reactions; it has enormous destructive power. Nuclear weapons have been used only twice for war, by the USA in Hiroshima and Nagasaki. However, they have been used many hundreds of times in nuclear testing undertaken by some countries. The declared nuclear powers are the USA, Russia, the United Kingdom, France, the People's Republic of China, and now Israel, India and Pakistan.

orbit the course of a celestial object or spacecraft around a star or planet

Patriot a medium-range surface-to-air missile system, developed in the USA

payload the part of a vehicle's load from which revenue (or purpose) is derived, e.g. cargo (a) an explosive warhead carried by a missile or aircraft, (b) personnel, equipment or satellites carried by a spacecraft

Prithvi a surface-to-surface battlefield missile

probe an unmanned exploratory spacecraft designed to transmit information about its environment

propellant a substance, fuel, that causes something to move or be driven forward

prototype a first or preliminary model of a machine, from which other models are developed

radar a system that detects the presence, direction, distance and speed of aircraft, and other objects, by sending out pulses of high-frequency electromagnetic waves which are reflected off the object and back to the source (from **ra**dio **de**tection **a**nd **r**anging)

recruitment   the action of enlisting personnel, usually for the armed forces

remote sensing   the scanning of the earth by satellites or high-flying aircraft, to gain information

reverse engineering   the reproduction of another manufacturer's product following detailed examination of its construction and composition; not originally produced

runway   a strip of specially designed ground, from which aircraft take off and land

satellite   an artificial body placed in orbit around the earth in order to collect information, or for communication

Scud   a short-range surface-to-surface ballistic missile, developed by the USSR

self-reliance   relying upon one's own powers and resources, rather than those of others

Shiva temple in Rameswaram   This temple is considered to be one of the holiest shrines of the Hindus. It is associated closely with the *Ramayana*. Legend has it that Rama worshipped Shiva in this spot after his victorious return from Lanka. The ancient temple is known for its long, ornate corridors and towers.
Shri Sita Rama Kalyana is the ritual wedding of Rama and Sita that is enacted at the shrine.

sovereignty   the authority of a country to govern itself or to govern another country

state-of-the-art   the most recent stage in the development of a product incorporating the newest ideas and the most up-to-date features

strategic   carefully designed or planned, and relating to the gaining of a military advantage (often contrasted with *tactical*)

stratified   to arrange into strata, or layers

sub-contract   employ a firm or organisation outside of one's own organisation to work on one part of a larger project

subsystem   a self-contained system within a larger system

sun-synchronous orbit a satellite in earth orbit that remains constant in relation to the sun; one advantage of a sun-synchronous orbit is that a spacecraft's solar arrays are in almost continuous sunlight, enabling it to primarily rely on solar rather than battery power

surface-to-air missile a missile designed to be fired from the ground at an aircraft

surface-to-surface missile a missile designed to be fired from one point on the ground or craft, at another such point or craft

tactical careful planning to achieve a specific military end (often contrasted with *strategic*)

telecommand the use of radio communication for the transmission of signals to a space station in order to initiate, modify or terminate functions of equipment on an associated space object

telemetry the practice of recording the readings of an instrument and transmitting them by radio

test range a range or area for conducting tests

tracking instruments instruments that maintain the constant difference in frequency between two or more connected circuits or components

trajectory the path of a flying missile or projectile

Trishul a short-range, quick-reaction surface-to-air missile

warhead the explosive head of a missile or similar weapon

wind tunnel a tunnel-like structure that produces an airstream of known velocity past models of aircraft, in order to investigate the flow or effect of wind on the full-size object

World War II (1939–45) This was among the most extensive and costly armed conflicts in world history. It involved a majority of nations, and was fought simultaneously in several parts of the world, resulting in the loss of approximately 55 million lives. The war was fought between two groups of powers—the alliance of the British Commonwealth, the USA, the USSR, China, and the governments-in-exile of France, Poland, and other occupied European countries, collectively known as the Allies or Allied forces; and Germany, Italy, and Japan and their allies, collectively known as the Axis powers.

DISTINCTIVE BOOKS FROM UNIVERSITIES PRESS

Vignettes in Physics

Bhabha and His Magnificent Obsessions	G Venkataraman
Bose and His Statistics	G Venkataraman
Chandrasekhar and His Limit	G Venkataraman
Raman and His Effect	G Venkataraman
Saha and His Formula	G Venkataraman

Scientists in 90 minutes

Scientists in 90 minutes	John & Mary Gribbin
Curie in 90 minutes	John & Mary Gribbin
Darwin in 90 minutes	John & Mary Gribbin
Einstein in 90 minutes	John & Mary Gribbin
Faraday in 90 minutes	John & Mary Gribbin
Galileo in 90 minutes	John & Mary Gribbin
Halley in 90 minutes	John & Mary Gribbin
Mendel in 90 minutes	John & Mary Gribbin
Newton in 90 minutes	John & Mary Gribbin

Makers of Modern Science

Charles Darwin: Evolution of a Naturalist	R Milner
Enrico Fermi: Pioneer of the Atomic Age	T Gottfried
James Watson and Francis Crick: Discovery of the Double Helix and Beyond	DE Newton
Jonas Salk	V Sherrow
The Leakey Family: Leaders in the Search for Human Origins	D Willis
Linus Pauling: Scientist and Advocate	DE Newton
Niels Bohr: Gentle Genius of Denmark	R Spangenburg & DK Moser
Robert Hutchings Goddord: Pioneer of Rocketry and Space Flight	SM Coil
Robert Oppenheimen Dark Prince	J Rummel
Wernher von Braun: Space Visionary and Rocket Engineer	R Spangenburg & DK Moser

On the Shoulders of Giants

The History of Science from the Ancient Greeks to the Scientific Revolution	R Spangenburg & DK Moser
The History of Science in the Eighteenth Century	R Spangenburg & DK Moser
The History of Science in the Nineteenth Century	R Spangenburg & DK Moser
The History of Science from 1895 to 1945	R Spangenburg & DK Moser
The History of Science from 1946 to the 1990s	R Spangenburg & DK Moser

Some Reference Books

An Imaginary Tale: The Story of Square Root of -1	PJ Nahin
Best Science Writing: Readings and Insight	R Gannon
Brief History of the Future	J Naughton
Concepts in Space Science	RR Daniel (ed)
é: The Story of a Number	E Maor
Explorations in Mathematics	AA Hattangadi
Fast Science Facts	Surendra Verma
Fun and Fundamentals of Mathematics	M Narlikar & J Narlikar
How to Enjoy Calculus	ES Pine
Indian Astronomy: An Introduction	S Balachandra Rao
Making a Clock-Accurate Sundial	S Muller
Milestones in Science and Technology: The Ready Reference Guide to Discoveries, Inventions and Facts	E Mount & BA List
Mysterious Motions and Other Intriguing Phenomena in Physics	GS Ranganath
New Unesco Source Book for Science Teaching	UNESCO
Planet Earth: The View from Space	J Baker
Science Matters: Principles of Science Simply Explained	R Hazen & J Trefil
Understanding Chemistry	CNR Rao
Understanding Chemistry CD	CNR Rao
Understanding Mathematics	KB Sinha et al
Universities Press Dictionary of Mathematics	J Daintith & JOE Clark
Universities Press Dictionary of Physics	J Daintith & JOE Clark